Outrageous
MERCY

Outrageous
MERCY

Rediscover the Radical Nature of Christianity

Wm. P.
FARLEY

BakerBooks
A Division of Baker Book House Co
Grand Rapids, Michigan 49516

© 2004 by Wm. P. Farley

Published by Baker Books
a division of Baker Book House Company
P.O. Box 6287, Grand Rapids, MI 49516-6287
www.bakerbooks.com

Printed in the United States of America

Library of Congress Cataloging-in-Publication Data
Farley, William P., 1948-
    Outrageous mercy : rediscover the radical nature of Christianity / William
P. Farley.
        p.   cm.
    Includes bibliographical references.
    ISBN 0-8010-6492-9 (pbk.)
    1. Theology, Doctrinal. I. Title.
BT75.3.F37 2004
230—dc22   2003022112

I would like to dedicate this book to my best friend, the woman who has shared all my hopes and dreams, who has been yoked with me in the gospel since 1973, and with whom God made me one flesh in 1971.

Her name does not appear on the cover, but it should. For without her support and encouragement, this book would not have been written. When I left a lucrative career to pursue writing and pastoral work, she heard the voice of God, stepped out in faith, and supported me, suppressing her love of security and her fear of financial loss for the greater glory of God. When I have felt fainthearted and despondent, she has been my daily encourager. She has shared my burden for the work. She has read and critiqued these pages with her uncanny common sense.

Judy, this book is the joint effort of, in the words of my friend Robert Andrews, a "one-flesh fighting machine." Thank you for yoking yourself with me in God's work so many years ago. Thank you for sharing my passion for the cross of Christ.

Contents

God hides His power in weakness,
His wisdom in folly,
His goodness in severity,
His justice in sins,
His mercy in His wrath.

Martin Luther

Acknowledgments

I would like to thank my parents, who patiently persevered as I underachieved through high school with a straight *C* average. (I barely passed my literature and creative writing classes.) I was a classic late bloomer. They probably didn't think I would get into college, let alone graduate. Thanks, Dad and Mom, for not giving up.

Second, I would like to thank the Rev. David Knight, who patiently mentored me in the Christian life for many years. May this book be some indication that his many efforts were not completely in vain.

Third, I would like to acknowledge the late Rev. Ern Baxter. It was from him that I first heard of the Puritans, the Reformers, and the riches of Reformed theology. His enthusiastic quotations from these men led me to buy the works of Jonathan Edwards and then those of the many other great Christian thinkers who have so profoundly influenced this manuscript. May he look down from Glory and rejoice.

Fourth, I want to thank Nikki Anderson. Her writing class at the local junior college (and her helpful editing) convinced me that I could learn to write.

Fifth, Sue Kline at *Discipleship Journal* published some of my articles and gave me the confidence to continue.

And last, the irrepressible enthusiasm and encouragement of Christine Tangvald kept me at the task of marketing this manuscript. (I almost gave up.) Thank you, Christine.

Preface

We have a wistful longing for simplicity, but in our busy world, many ideas compete for our attention. And the Bible is a complex book, interpreted differently by sincere, believing Christians. Is there a way to distill the essential Christian message out of the nonessential theological debris? And if so, where does the Bible speak these truths in simple, uncluttered pictures?

Everything Christians really need to know about life is not learned in kindergarten, as one well-known book suggests. Instead, Christians learn these lessons at the cross. The cross teaches us everything we need to know about life, death, God, humanity, eternity, and a host of other issues.

The first thing every aspiring writer learns is "show, don't tell." In other words, don't lecture your readers, but "show" your points and premises with stories, anecdotes, quotes, and dialogue. The cross is God's "show, don't tell." Systematic theologies catalog and systematize the Bible's doctrines, and their work is important—but they "tell" us the truth. The cross shows us.

The cross has two dimensions. It is something God has *done for us*, but it is also a revelation of vital truths *communicated to us*.

When we think of the cross we usually think of the former, what God has done for us. He has reconciled us to himself. He has purchased forgiveness for all who believe and repent. He has absorbed the wrath of God on our behalf. He has loved us with an everlasting love.

But the emphasis of this book will be on the latter—what the cross says to us. As John Stott noted, "Through what God did there *for* the world he was also speaking *to* the world. Just as human beings disclose their character in their actions, so God has shown himself to us in the death of His Son."[1]

When we focus on the cross, the basics become simple and clear.

My interest in this subject is a matter of profound grace, for which I will always be grateful. Fifteen years after my conversion I purchased the works of Jonathan Edwards. To this day I don't remember why, except that I had heard Ern Baxter mention Edwards in his preaching. And for the first time I began to see the cross, what it says, and what it stands for. I had always believed in the cross, but like many contemporary Christians, I did not understand its message except on a very basic, superficial level.

With impeccable logic Edwards enlarged many of the lessons taught by the cross. The thorough, biblical nature of his arguments stopped all my objections. I was deeply moved, shaken to my foundation, and painted into an intellectual corner from which I had no escape. I joyfully surrendered to the sweet knowledge of Edwards's immense God.

Then God led me to *A Harmony of the Divine Attributes* by Dr. William Bates, one of the sage Puritan divines. Bates examined how the cross synthesized and harmonized the wrath and love of God, the grace and justice of God, the law and mercy of God, etc. After reading these books, I began to look increasingly to the cross to unravel many theological lessons. The following chapters are the fruit of that quest.

This book is not a perfectly balanced theological treatise. Rather, it is an examination of some of the key messages spoken to us through Jesus' death. I say "some" because it would take several volumes to discuss them all in detail.

Furthermore, the subjects taken up by each chapter are not exhaustively dealt with in those chapters. For instance, the Bible tells us much more about waging spiritual warfare than what I have written in chapter 7. The purpose of each chapter is not to give an exhaustive teaching on that subject, but to examine some of the salient truths the cross teaches us.

My work will be worthwhile, and I will be satisfied, if you finish this volume longing to plunge more deeply into the implications of the cross for everyday life. You will never reach the end of its lessons and ramifications in this life or eternity.

May God bless your reading, stirring a hunger to know more perfectly what Paul called simply "the message of the cross" (1 Cor. 1:18).

I

The Centrality of the Cross

No theology is genuinely Christian which does not arise from and focus on the cross.

Martin Luther

I had a long layover while waiting for a connecting flight at a California airport, so I decided to take the fifteen-minute drive north to tour a major university campus. I was greeted by a ten-foot totem pole dedicated to "All Humankind" as I crossed the campus. Then, to enter the student bookstore, I had to run a gauntlet of homosexual literature, feminist books, and radical environmental propaganda strategically placed at the front entrance. I felt like a stranger in a foreign land.

I decided to go to the library to do some reading. A jovial, middle-aged employee with a long gray ponytail stopped me at the entrance. He must have sensed that I needed directions. Around his neck on a leather string hung a large wooden cross.

"Are you a Christian?" I asked, nodding hopefully toward his cross.

He fingered it, paused for a second, then looked at me with a knowing smile. "You bet I am. I love the Man that died on this for me."

We shared our faith for a minute, shook hands, and parted. *God always has his seven thousand who have not bowed their knee to Baal,* I thought. *What an encouragement to meet a brother in this hostile environment.* The man's cross was our point of contact.

The Centrality of the Cross

The cross is more than a symbol connecting two Christians in a hostile environment. It is the heart and soul of our faith. The cross alone is our theology, wrote Martin Luther, a remarkably prescient thinker.[1]

In other words, what the heart is to the body, the cross is to our faith. What the foundation is to a building, the cross is to Christian thought and practice. Lay this doctrine crooked, and our faith will be a Leaning Tower of Pisa.

The cross is also the motor of the Christian worldview. That is why Dr. James Denney wrote in 1903:

> It will be admitted by most Christians that if the Atonement [the cross] . . . is anything to the mind, it is everything. It is the most profound of all truths. . . . It determines more than anything else our conceptions of God, of man, of history. . . . It is the inspiration of all thought, the impulse and the law of all action, the key, in the last resort, to all suffering. . . . It is the focus of revelation, the point at which we see deepest into the truth of God, and come most completely under its power. . . . It is Christianity in brief; it concentrates in itself, as in a germ of infinite potency, all that the wisdom, power and love of God mean in relation to sinful men.[2]

Some think that the cross is a basic doctrine learned in the early stages of our spiritual development so that we can advance to the deeper mysteries as we mature. But the cross is the deeper truth. There is nothing deeper. It is a bottomless well, a fountain of vibrant truth, and a pinnacle of wisdom and knowledge. In it lie the depths of the mysteries of God. The first sign of spiritual maturity is when one increasingly thinks about, ponders, marvels, and wonders at the mystery of the cross.

The Cross Matters

The message of the cross matters to us for at least four reasons.

First, the cross is our message. It is the heart, soul, and center of Christian faith and practice. There is no good news apart from the cross. The ensuing chapters will argue that almost every subject addressed is enlightened by reference to the cross. It is the manual to which all Christians should turn to fill their spiritual tank, resolve every ethical question, and amplify every doctrine. Does this sound like an exaggeration? It is not. It is an understatement.

For this reason, powerful preaching is usually cross-centered. Not just evangelistic preaching, but teaching to provoke holiness, to strengthen family life, to motivate stewardship, and to advance every other subject of Christian interest. The cross is the socket into which the preacher plugs for power to illuminate these subjects.

When Christian culture, politics, church government, Calvinism,[3] health and wealth, or the "baptism in the Holy Spirit" become our message, we suffer. I speak from experience. Many of these things have distracted me.

Of course, these doctrines have a place at the table. And they are helpful—if their place is secondary. But when they become central in our focus, they turn our thoughts to this world. By contrast, the cross turns our thoughts to heaven. These doctrines bend our minds to ourselves and our needs, but the cross rivets our gaze on God and his sufficiency. These doctrines puff up our contentiousness, but the cross breaks us, making us meek, gracious, and humble. These doctrines obscure the love of God, but the cross magnifies it in our experience. These doctrines distract us from personal holiness, but the cross motivates us to be holy as God is holy.

Second, the cross is our teacher. The cross is a window through which we learn everything we need to know about God, humanity, wisdom, worship, the purpose of suffering, the purpose of life, and a host of other issues. If you knew nothing else but the cross, but you knew it thoroughly, you would know everything essential for this life and the next. That is not to say that the rest of the Bible is unnecessary. But it is to say that the cross displays for us all the essential teaching of the Bible in vivid terms. The message of the Bible is more than the message of the cross, but it is never less.

Third, the power of God is in the cross, and we desperately need God's power. That is why Paul wrote, "I resolved to know nothing while I was with you except Jesus Christ and him crucified. . . . My message and my preaching were not with wise and persuasive words, but with a demonstration of the Spirit's power" (1 Cor. 2:2, 4). Paul knew how to get results. He understood that God's power is in the proclamation of the cross, because the cross displays God's character and our immense need.

For this reason, the preaching of the cross often initiates revival. "For the message of the cross is foolishness to those who are perishing, but to us who are being saved it is the *power of God*" (1 Cor. 1:18, emphasis mine), wrote one who experienced that power daily. This message shakes nations and converts multitudes. It takes great courage to proclaim it, and we must proclaim it, because a Christianity that does not understand and boldly preach the cross is cowardly, powerless, and unfocused. It is flavorless salt.

After studying in great detail the history of revival, Brian Edwards notes:

The emphasis on the blood of Christ as the way of salvation has never been popular. . . . In revival, Christ, and the blood of the cross particularly, is central to the preaching. . . . In the eighteenth century Whitefield and Wesley found that the preaching of the cross was hated, just as it is hated now. But thousands found in the blood of Christ justification, redemption, propitiation, peace, reconciliation and cleansing, whether or not they understood all those terms.

Joseph Kemp returned from a visit to Wales in 1905 (during the Welsh Revival) and reported to his congregation at Charlotte Chapel in Edinburgh that the dominating note of the Welsh revival was "redemption through the Blood." Whenever we hear or read that the Spirit is at work we can assess the genuineness of the work by how central the blood of Christ is to the preaching and the worship.[4]

If we want the refreshing rains of God's Spirit to fall, we must restore this message to prominence. The power of God flows through it and from it.

Fourth, the presence or absence of cross-centeredness impacts behavior. Christianity that is not cross-centered will be sympathy without decisiveness, kindness without justice, charm without backbone, and sentimentality without action.

Christianity then becomes a religion for the deserving but not for sinners, a message for the upper-class but not the lower-class. Without the cross, justification by faith alone degenerates into moralism, and God's holy wrath morphs into tolerance for the well-intentioned. A cross-less Christianity tames the terrible God enthroned between the cherubim before whom the nations tremble (Ps. 99:1). God becomes love, but nothing else. In short, when the message of the cross is removed from the center of Christianity, Christianity removes itself from the center of our thoughts and devotions. A bushel basket is placed over the lamp. It is that simple.

Most importantly, cross-centered Christians grow progressively humble. I fellowship with one church that preaches the cross. They sing it, they preach it, they read about it, and they exult in it. Therefore, they feel deeply their sinfulness and unworthiness. Humility is their outstanding quality.

Another church in my area believes in the cross, but transforming the culture is their central focus. They write about culture, sing about it, and discuss it constantly. By contrast, their outstanding quality is pride. They look down on other Christians. They are contentious and lack grace.

Therefore, our attitude toward the cross is crucial. When its importance recedes in our thoughts and affections, we become cold, sterile, and lifeless. But when the message of the cross takes center stage, we burn with zeal for God and his kingdom from a deep sense of our spiritual poverty.

Taking the Cross for Granted

If you are like me, though, you have probably taken the cross for granted. Then we are like the second church just mentioned. The cross is on our sign and over our sanctuary, but we never think or talk about it. As P. T. Forsyth observed in 1908, when that happens, "we are merely running the kingdom . . . without the cross—with the cross perhaps on our sign, but not in our centre. We have the old trade mark, but what does that matter in a dry and thirsty land where no water is, if the artesian well on our premises is going dry?"[5]

Reasons for Neglecting Christ's Message

The artesian well of the Christian faith is the proclamation of Christ crucified and the vital truths for which this message

20

stands. It is easy to neglect the message, and we do so for several reasons.

First, we neglect the cross because its sheer familiarity numbs us to the reality of the critical truths for which it stands. As Forsyth noted, it becomes just a "trade mark." Crosses sit atop church steeples and mark graveyards. Basketball players make the sign of the cross before they shoot free throws. Crosses emblazon ambulances hurrying by in rush-hour traffic. Drug companies put crosses on pill bottles. Crosses adorn our hospitals and relief agencies. Movie stars wear diamond-studded crosses on necklaces or earrings. Some people even plant crosses on highways where fatal accidents have occurred.

The amazing fact is that despite our secularism, the symbol of the cross is still all around us, speaking mercy, compassion, and healing. It is a symbol of hope and virtue. "No word in human language has become more universally known than this word [the cross]," notes *The International Standard Bible Encyclopaedia.* "And that because all of the history of the world since the death of Christ has been measured by the distance which separates events from it."[6]

In this case, the old saying can be true: "Familiarity breeds contempt." The ubiquitous presence of the cross in Western culture numbs us to its piercing, life-changing truths. This frequency deafens us to its message, much like when we see a commercial too many times.

Second, we neglect the cross because we don't clearly understand it. I remember a men's conference I once attended at which an admired friend was asked to speak about the cross. I came with high expectations, but he gave three messages that were confusing, powerless, and unconvincing. He had been a church leader for thirty years, and he was a good teacher, so how could he speak so lifelessly on such a vital message? He only understood the cross on a superficial level, and this is a common problem for many.

Third, we neglect the cross because it offends. A friend from a large, seeker-friendly church recently boasted that his congregation had removed the cross from their sanctuary. To him it was an embarrassment and an impediment to evangelism. This embarrassment is both a symptom of and a reason for our complacency. When some see the offense, God's pristine holiness and hatred of evil, and the depth of humanity's sinfulness, they turn their backs on the cross's scandalous message. But the message of the cross will always be "foolish" and "scandalous" to the mind of unbelief. Even after New Birth, we may have a substantial element of this "foolishness" still residing in us, making it possible to still be deeply "offended" by the word of the cross. Neither you, nor I, are immune from this problem.

Once we see its offensiveness, the cost of identifying with it becomes apparent. I remember a Christian brother who once told me, "I can tolerate anything except being misunderstood. I hate to be misunderstood." But those who really understand and proclaim the cross will be misunderstood. Right after Jesus explained the cross to his disciples (Luke 9:23–24), he warned, "If anyone is ashamed of me and my words, the Son of Man will be ashamed of him when he comes in his glory and in the glory of the Father and of the holy angels" (Luke 9:26). Jesus knew the message of the cross would embarrass. It was this "offense" that caused most of Paul's persecutions and sufferings. So if no one is persecuting you, you probably haven't grasped this message sufficiently to offend anyone yet.

Embarrassment about the cross is embarrassment about Christ himself; we cannot separate our feelings about Jesus and our feelings about his cross. "Christ is to us just what his cross is," noted P. T. Forsyth. "All that Christ was in heaven or on earth was put into what he did there. . . . Christ, I repeat, is to us just what his cross is. You do not understand Christ till you understand his cross."[7]

We can't despise the gift and admire the giver. The cross was God's great gift. The wonderful Being who died there was infinite in value and dignity. In return for the lavish expenditure of an infinite life, God rightfully expects our devotion. That is why no one can take his cross for granted and at the same time love him properly.

We may claim fervency about the cross, but our behavior speaks our real feelings. We are what we do, not what we say. For instance, my wife is God's greatest earthly gift to me. But after fifteen years of marriage, I began to take her cooking, housecleaning, washing, and mothering of our children for granted. She interpreted my apathy about what she *did* for apathy about herself, and as a result she felt hurt and unimportant. So I confessed my sin and asked her forgiveness.

In a far more significant way, we grieve God's Spirit when we take his cross—his great act of servant-love—for granted. And we are all guilty, at least to some extent, of this sin.

Symptoms of Apathy

Apathy about the cross has clear symptoms. The first is that we just never think about it. We think about evangelism, church growth, prayer, the Bible, God's mercy, maybe even God's love, our friends, or our jobs, but we seldom meditate upon and delight in the cross itself. Imagine selling everything you owned to purchase a diamond ring for your beloved, only to have her bury it in a box and never wear it. That is what we unknowingly do with God when we fail to make the cross the center of our thought life.

A second symptom of cross apathy is legalism. We know what to do, but we don't know why we should do it or how to handle failure when it occurs. For many years I attended a church with strong teaching on practical holiness. We emphasized holiness in relating to our families, handling money, serving God with our time, and serving our employers. Our genuine desire for holiness was Spirit-inspired, but we didn't understand what should motivate holiness or how to handle failure. Therefore, our teaching manipulated people into holiness by appealing to duty and the guilt that followed when they failed. But the cross pulls us into holiness for the right reasons and salves our consciences when we fail. The cross produces spiritual disciplines responding to grace rather than guilt.

Our prayer life is the third important barometer for apathy. When our church gathers for prayer and we don't issue heartfelt prayers of thanksgiving, exultation, and praise for Christ's work on the cross, it is because the cross is not at the center of our affections. For many of us, the cross is an afterthought. We pour out our needs and then conclude, "And thank you for dying for my sins."

The Bible calls cross-centered prayer the "new song." It is the song of redemption that the Holy Spirit teaches every true believer in varying degrees. This song is a deep and profound sense of gratitude for our deliverance from sin, hell, guilt, and the wrath of God. It is always a response of exuberant joy to God's saving work. "He lifted me out of the slimy pit, out of the mud and mire; he set my feet on a rock and gave me a firm place to stand. He put a *new song* in my mouth, a hymn of praise to our God" (Ps. 40:2–3, emphasis mine).

We learn the new song to the degree that we are deeply enamored by the cross. It cannot be suppressed in one amazed at God's saving work—anyone who knows this joy will pray it regularly from a sense of personal unworthiness.

A fourth symptom is leaders who do not preach the cross with power—as if they see and feel the dreadful realities of heaven and hell revealed there. Those who really see the message of the cross will preach like Richard Baxter: "I preached as never sure to preach, and as a dying man to dying men."[8]

A fifth symptom of cross apathy is when there is little mourning for sin in our midst. "They will look on me, the one they have pierced," prophesied Zechariah. "And they will mourn for him as one mourns for an only child, and grieve bitterly for him as one grieves for a firstborn son" (Zech. 12:10). To the degree that we really see the message of the cross we will be stricken, deeply stricken for our sins, the sins of our church, and the sins of the nation in which we live. To the degree that the cross does not speak to us there will be little mourning for sin and its consequences. "Blessed are those who mourn, for they will be comforted" (Matt. 5:4).

A sixth symptom of cross apathy is the lack of a growing spiritual capacity to embrace the love of God. The most common complaint I hear from Christians is that they wish they experienced the love of God more fully. The cross is the cure. The absence of a heartfelt experience of God's love usually points to a dearth of preaching and meditating on the cross. "We love because he first loved us" (1 John 4:19). "This is how we know what love is: Jesus Christ laid down his life for us" (1 John 3:16).

The lyrical content of our worship music is a seventh symptom. An article by Mark Noll in *Christianity Today* titled "We Are What We Sing" sums up an important principle. Music reflects what we value and reveals what we really think about. In fact, our music usually sings the truths most important to us.[9]

A friend just went through several hundred worship songs from a church he used to attend. The tunes were good, and the lyrics extolled God's greatness, his holiness, his love and mercy, and the importance of his lordship. But there was not one song that specifically and exclusively spoke about the work of Christ at the cross. Significantly, none mentioned our sinfulness and depravity or the fact that we deserve judgment but instead received amazing grace. The church that this music came from believed in human sinfulness and the atoning work of Christ at the cross. But these lyrics revealed how little they understood and valued these truths. Worship is a response to the goodness of God revealed at the cross. A collection of music with little cross emphasis will dilute our worship from the high purpose God intends.

My friend's worship experience could be duplicated in many churches today. To find cross-centered lyrics, you often have to go back two or three hundred years to hymns written during times of profound revival, when God had bared his holy arm, exposing the church to the profundity of the cross. It is a sad indictment that the church writes very little cross-centered music today.[10]

Conclusion

Cross apathy has a price. If some or all of these symptoms describe you or your church, you need the following chapters. But before we go to those chapters and describe some of the lessons taught by the cross, let's examine six foundational principles apart from which the following chapters cannot be understood.

2

Foundations

> He that intends to build high lays the foundation deep and low.
>
> John Flavel

A successful sports personality in our area is building a beauti-ful home on the edge of a cliff that has a panoramic view of the surrounding area. As I write this, the builder is pouring and crafting the foundations. He has taken great care on this part of the project because the structure will only be as secure as its underpinning. This is especially true since the house perches on the edge of a cliff.

The doctrine of the cross sits on a cliff of doctrinal seduction. If the foundations are not strong, it will easily slide off into the impotence of error. There are at least six foundational truths that support any teaching about the cross.

The Great Divide

Our response to the cross is the great divide of religion. It, more than anything else, reveals the nature of our relationship to God. The confession that Jesus died on a cross, that he is God, and that his death is an atonement for sin is *the* crucial fact of history. Either it is true or it isn't.

Two Mormon missionaries pedaled down my driveway one day. I put on a smile and a prayer and went out to greet them. After a few pleasantries I got down to the basics. "In your opinion, was Jesus Christ equal with the Father?"

They thought about it for a minute. "No, he was the son of God. He was not equal with God."

"You've probably never thought of it this way," I said gently, "but unless the person sacrificed on the cross was truly God, your sins and mine are not forgiven. Our sin is so serious in God's sight that only a divine sacrifice was valuable enough to right God's scale of justice, cleanse our consciences, and atone for the infinite offense of sin."

"We don't agree that sin is that serious, or that Jesus was God," they answered. And they got back on their bicycles and rode off.

There is great confusion about the cross, and the devil likes it that way. Both Mormons and Jehovah's Witnesses believe that Jesus died on a cross but that he was not God. Most Muslims do not believe that Jesus died on a cross; they believe that at the last minute the Jews substituted another in his place. Most Jews believe he died on a cross but that he was just a wannabe prophet. He was not God's Son; therefore, his death had no significance. Eastern religions believe that Jesus was a son of God, but that he was not unique. There have been many sons of God. And he did not die to atone for sin because God is impersonal. God does not care about sin.

Here is where non-Christian religions stumble. They either believe that Jesus died on a cross but that he was just a good man, or they believe that he died some other way. They believe that he was a son of God in the same way that every man is a son of God, or they believe that he died but not to propitiate the wrath of God stirred up by sin. But if the man crucified was the Lord

28

of the universe clothed in human flesh, who died for sin, then everything changes.

A Historic Event

Jesus' death on the cross is a historic event, not some vapid spiritual idealization.

I was talking with an unbelieving friend about the claims of Christianity. It was a friendly conversation, but it was going nowhere. Finally, I said, "Do you believe that Jesus died and rose from the dead?"

My friend paused. She thought hard. Finally, she carefully answered. "You know, I don't think I believe that. It is just too fantastic to me."

I knew then that I was plowing where God was not sowing. The cross is historical fact.

History stands on the testimony of eyewitnesses. Many witnessed the conquests of Alexander the Great. Many witnessed the reign of Augustus Caesar. We weren't there, but we believe these events occurred because many people witnessed them. In the same way, Jesus' death is a historical fact. Hundreds witnessed it. More than five hundred witnessed his resurrection (I Cor. 15:6), and most of them suffered terribly for that testimony. There is no doubt that Jesus Christ lived in Galilee and died in Jerusalem. Compared to the fact of the cross, Alexander, Augustus Caesar, and the great empires of history are like a dream that one forgets upon awakening. But the glory of Christ's cross will become increasingly real and substantial as we plow into eternity.

If the Son of God really died for our sins at Calvary, then the cross is the central, crowning event in time and space. It should be the chief object of our study and the supreme object of our delight, beside which all else is trivial.

Details of Crucifixion

Crucifixion was a nasty way to die. There is almost no way to exaggerate its brutality. Even the cruel, ruthless Roman government crucified only the lowest social classes—slaves and commoners. A Roman citizen could be beheaded for a capital crime but never crucified. Because Paul was a Roman citizen he was probably beheaded, but Peter, a commoner, was crucified (upside down, according to legend). The cross was so distasteful that Cicero said it should never be mentioned in polite company. To the Jews it was a sign of God's cursing. It was a breathtakingly humiliating death, which usually took place near garbage dumps or similarly degraded locations.

The victim was nailed or tied to a cross that was then impaled into the ground. The condemned was left to die a slow death from thirst and exposure. It was lingering, agonizing torture, and because the loss of blood was minimal, death usually took several days. The fastest recorded deaths were after thirty-six hours. In some cases, the executioners broke the victims' legs, crushed their ribs, or scourged them to hasten death. They showed Jesus this mercy.

Convulsions usually set in, and each movement tore the victim's hands and feet against the raw wounds.[1] The pain was excruciating. Because the offender cried out for death, soldiers were stationed around the cross to prevent friends from killing the convicted or freeing him by force.

To enhance the humiliation, the malefactor often was crucified naked. The authorities usually nailed a placard over the cross, broadcasting the crime for which the criminal suffered. It might read "stealing," "murder," or "insurrection." In Jesus' case it read, "King of the Jews." He was crucified for telling the truth.

God, who is sovereign, sent his Son into a culture where the barbarity of crucifixion was practiced. He did this to make a point.

He could have sent Jesus to twenty-first-century North America, where we execute capital criminals by painless lethal injection. But God sent Jesus to ancient Rome and a cross because that was the only death that would accomplish the job for which the Father sent him. He had to suffer infinite pains to atone for an infinite weight of sin and to express his Father's infinite hatred for sin.

Substitution

Fourth, the cross was a satisfaction of God's justice made by a substitute. Theologians call this the penal, substitutionary atonement. It means that Jesus went to the cross in our place, as our substitute. He took our sin upon himself, and because sin deserves God's wrath, he bore crucifixion to exhaust the wrath that stood against us. He suffered the terrible penalty of sin that we deserved, and in the process satisfied the demands of God's justice. "God made him who had no sin to be sin for us, so that in him we might become the righteousness of God" (2 Cor. 5:21).

He also lived a perfect life, and by so doing substituted his righteousness for our lack. When we believe, God imputes his holy perfection (righteousness) to us.

In summary, Jesus' death satisfied God's need for justice, and his life satisfied our need for righteousness. It was a two-way substitution. Our sins were imputed to Christ so that his righteousness could be imputed to us.

Substitution should not surprise us. John Stott has observed that both sin and redemption involve substitution. The essence of Adam's sin was that he substituted himself for God. He elevated himself—desiring to be like God. "You will be like God, knowing good and evil" (Gen. 3:5). But Jesus turned the tables. When he went to the cross, God substituted himself for sinful man. In this self-humbling, God greatly glorified himself, lavishing infinite love on unworthy creatures.

I remember trying to explain this concept to my grade-school children. The next day my son, David, got in trouble. When my second daughter, Anne, heard about it, she came to me and said, "Dad, I want to take David's spanking in his place." Understanding the substitutionary atonement, she was deeply moved at what Jesus had done for her. Although I explained that she could not take her brother's punishment, I was secretly delighted by her insight. The Holy Spirit had communicated the wonder and reality of the substitutionary atonement to a nine-year-old. In her simplicity, Anne grasped what many middle-aged theologians don't.

The church has found the substitutionary atonement difficult to hang on to. It is a slippery doctrine. Within one generation of the apostles' death it was almost lost.[2] For fourteen hundred years, with the exception of a few short revivals,[3] it lay dormant. Sincere men developed other theories to explain the cross, but none of them satisfied the full biblical testimony on this subject. Only with the Reformation and its emphasis on the Bible did the doctrine reemerge in a blaze of full glory.

Even though both the Old and New Testaments testify to it explicitly,[4] not all Christians today accept the substitutionary atonement. There are many reasons for this, but the most common is its offensiveness. The substitutionary atonement testifies to the depths of our sin and helplessness, and to the righteousness of God's wrath and the holiness of his justice.

Why is it that a doctrine so crucial to our spiritual health is so hard to hang on to? It is because the power of God is in it! The devil hates it, and human pride despises it. Both war against it incessantly, so it takes a mighty display of God's power to advance and maintain this truth in the church. Therefore, it behooves us to protect the doctrine of the cross jealously, specifically the substitutionary atonement, soberly aware that the winds of pride and unbelief will easily wither it.

Ensuing chapters will examine this doctrine in more detail. But it is enough here to state its importance. The acceptance or rejection of the substitutionary atonement is a great divide separating authentic Christians from those who play games with the Bible. "It is the recognition of this divine necessity [the satisfaction of God's wrath and justice by the cross]," noted Dr. Denney, "or the failure to recognize it, which ultimately divides interpreters of Christianity into evangelical and nonevangelical, those who are true to the New Testament and those who cannot digest it."[5]

A Display of Goodness

Fifth, God displayed all of his moral goodness on the cross. The goodness of God revealed in the Old Testament was a candle, but the cross was a blazing sun of glory. "For in the cross of Christ, as in a splendid theatre, the incomparable goodness of God is set before the whole world," noted John Calvin. "The glory of God shines, indeed, in all creatures on high and below, but never more brightly than in the cross."[6] Some insight into this goodness is essential to our New Birth.

Conversion begins when the light of God's moral goodness shines in our hearts. "For God, who said, 'Let light shine out of darkness,' made his light shine in our hearts to give us the light of the knowledge of the glory of God in the face of Christ" (2 Cor. 4:6). The cross is the full blazing forth of this glorious light. We need more than intellectual faith. The demons have that. "Even the demons believe that—and shudder" (James 2:19). Faith that saves *trusts* God. It is seated in the heart not the mind. It begins to see his goodness—and God revealed his goodness at the cross. Therefore, the proclamation of the cross is foundational for evangelism.

Sanctification also proceeds from a revelation of the goodness of God, and the cross is the best place to behold it. One who sees

33

God's goodness begins to trust him. And people who trust God put their lives at risk and begin to obey.

Therefore, the proclamation of the cross is crucial to saving faith and sanctification. "Faith comes from hearing the message, and the message is heard through the word of Christ" (Rom. 10:17). The message heard is the word of the cross and all it entails. This is why Paul wrote, "For I resolved to know nothing while I was with you except Jesus Christ and him crucified" (I Cor. 2:2). This gospel, and no other, is life for a dying world.

It Offends

Sixth, as we have already seen, God releases the power of the cross to the degree that we let it offend. And the message of the cross offends the pride of man. If we don't let the cross accomplish this humbling work, we rob God of his glory, because God delights in glorifying himself through the foolishness of this message. God has designed our salvation so that "no man might boast" in anything but Jesus Christ and him crucified. When our attempts to minimize the offense diminish God's glory, he often withdraws his power.

To many of us the cross is only about love. But the message of God's love is not what makes the message of the cross offensive. The cross speaks to us about human sin, the wrath we deserve, and the holiness of God. This is what made it "foolishness" to the Greek (I Cor. 1:23), the "smell of death" to the unconverted (2 Cor. 2:16), and an "offense" to the mind of even many new converts (Gal. 5:11). In fact, if you have never been deeply scandalized and offended by the cross, you may have never really heard its message. The powerful truth is that God hides his love, mercy, grace, and power in this scandal. We must rejoice in the offense to get these benefits.

Conclusion

We can know all about the cross, and we can believe in the cross, but we can also relegate it to a back shelf in our thoughts and priorities. This is Christianity on the decline. If it is true of you and your church, you can reverse this trend.

It is imperative that we do so. We can put the cross on the back shelf and still be Christians, but the slide will continue. The children of those who accept a Christianity centered in something other than the cross won't put the cross on the back shelf; they will put Christianity on the back shelf. And the next generation might even forget the faith altogether.

I knew all about Vienna before I went there. I read books about its history. I studied pictures of its great cathedrals. But everything changed after I spent a week there. Now I know Vienna from personal experience.

In the same way, I knew all about the cross for twenty years after my conversion. I understood and believed its message, at least on a basic level. I even taught it to others. But in my early forties the reality of its truths began to penetrate my mind and spirit. I began to know it in the same way that I know Vienna after walking its streets and eating its food.

The cross encourages every Christian to the degree that we understand its message. Each chapter that follows will attempt to show how the cross sheds light on one of life's basic problems or questions. Hopefully, you will continue to apply the lessons of the cross to additional areas of life long after you finish this book.

May God bless your reading.

3

God 101

All our troubles ultimately emanate from our ignorance
of God. . . .You will never know God as Father except by
Jesus Christ, and in particular, by his death upon the cross.
. . . Look there, gaze, meditate, survey the wondrous cross.
And then you will see something of him.

Dr. Martyn Lloyd-Jones

A W. Tozer observed that "what comes to mind when we
think about God is the most important thing about us."[1]
This is because we worship our idea of God, and that idea then
determines all that we think and do. Every one of us becomes
like the god we worship, whether it is self, success, the state, or
the living God revealed in the pages of the Bible.

I am no exception to this principle. When I thought of God's
love as primarily affection, I thought I had to feel good about
someone in order to love him or her. Because I thought that Jesus
died for us *because* we were his friends, I was unwilling to serve
anyone who was not my friend. Because I thought that Jesus loved
us because we are "good people," I looked down on those who

didn't quite measure up. The examples could go on and on. "No religion has ever been greater than its idea of God," continues Tozer. "Worship is pure or base as the worshipper entertains high or low thoughts of God."[2]

In my experience, many evangelicals worship a simplistic God woven together from the Bible, folklore, and pop psychology. If we suffer from spiritual shallowness, this mixture is probably the root cause.

Here's an example. I teach a men's Bible study. On the morning that John first joined us, we were studying the first three chapters of Romans. These chapters discuss the wrath of God often, so on this morning we did also.

Afterwards, John drew me aside. "Why are you so hung up on the wrath of God?" he asked. "My God is a God of love. I get depressed when you mention wrath. Modern Christians are too sophisticated to accept such an antiquated view of God. Besides, how can God be loving and wrathful at the same time? I don't get it."

Many of us can identify with John's frustration. In our search to answer his question, we either explain away large portions of Scripture or we find a way to reconcile biblically the wrath of God with his love. The cross, understood properly, resolves this dilemma in a way that is faithful to the entire Bible. In fact, the cross message synthesizes the Bible's divergent statements about God into one consistent message that satisfies even the most demanding intellect.

Solving this problem matters because knowing God is at the heart of everything important. In fact, it is eternal life. "This is eternal life: that they *know* you, the only true God, and Jesus Christ, whom you have sent" (John 17:3, emphasis added). This "knowing" begins with a right intellectual understanding of God. When the Holy Spirit reveals this knowledge to us, it becomes conviction written upon our hearts. We experience it.

Another way to say this is that at conversion, God lights a fire in our hearts. The fuel that sustains the flame is an accurate knowledge of God. When the Holy Spirit reaches into our minds for more fuel, and finds some, the fire intensifies. But where there is little or no fuel, the flame falters, sputters, and wanes.[3] Therefore, it is crucial that we entertain right ideas about God. Confusion here will cause much unwanted trouble elsewhere.

When I began to understand the cross fifteen years after my conversion, I began to understand why the apostles could write about the love and wrath of God and feel no contradiction.[4] The cross reveals one unchanging God who both visits sin with wrath and loves the unlovable with an inexpressible and glorious love.

The Presupposition

Reconciling justice and mercy is a conundrum to many. I thought about it seriously for the first time while watching the 1967 movie *Camelot*, which tells the story of King Arthur and his round table. The two people Arthur loved most, his queen, Guinevere, and his best friend, Lancelot, had fallen in love and betrayed him by committing adultery. Guinevere was found out, tried by a jury, convicted of treason, and condemned to burning at the stake.

The king was torn by his passion for justice and his desire to show Guinevere mercy. At the climax of the movie, as a soldier lights the wood under the queen's feet, a servant approaches a frustrated Arthur. "Your majesty, why not ignore the verdict and pardon her? But you can't do that, can you? If she dies your life is over. If she lives your life is a fraud. Kill the queen or kill the law."

Those were Arthur's choices. Kill the queen and uphold justice, or show Guinevere mercy and show the law, and justice, to be a fraud. To his great relief, the king was spared the choice, because Lancelot arrived, rescued the queen, and stole her away to safety.

God faced the same predicament, but there was no Lancelot to spare him. He loved sinful man, but he also loved justice. He could not just forgive man at the expense of justice and his law. He had to find a way to forgive sinners and satisfy justice at the same time. In the wisdom of God, the cross was the means to that end.

To understand how the cross reconciles God's wrath and love (justice and mercy) we must start by assuming that Christ's cross did two things. It displayed both God's justice and his love, and it reconciled them to each other. Wayne Grudem writes:

> What was the ultimate cause that led to Christ's coming to earth and dying for our sins? To find this we must trace the question back to something in the character of God himself. And here Scripture points to two things: the love and justice of God.[5]

If you asked the average Christian why Jesus died, the person might answer, "To reveal God's love" or "To save sinners." But when Paul thought about the cross, Christ's passion for justice came to mind first. Paul knew that we must understand God's love of justice before we can appreciate his immense love. Because of this, many theologians think Romans 3:25–26 is one of the pivotal verses in Romans.

> He did this [presented Christ Jesus as a sacrifice of atonement] to demonstrate his justice, because in his forbearance he had left the sins committed beforehand unpunished—he did it to demonstrate his justice at the present time, so as to be just and the one who justifies those who have faith in Jesus.

In other words, Paul is saying that first of all Jesus died to display God's justice and righteousness. His death also displayed his love. But because love cannot be discerned until we see his justice, Paul emphasizes God's justice first.

God's Zeal for Justice

The justice of God is the crucial starting place for any accurate understanding of Christ or his cross. God is just. "The LORD is our judge, the LORD is our lawgiver, the LORD is our king; it is he who will save us" (Isa. 33:22). But this is not where most of us start.

As a non-Christian lay dying, a friend asked what he was going to do about his sins. The man replied flippantly, "Don't worry. It is God's job to forgive." Many of us would agree with this statement because we think God is obligated to forgive.

But the cross says that forgiveness is not God's job. Instead, God's job is to be just and to execute justice perfectly. If forgiveness, grace, and mercy were required, they would no longer be forgiveness, grace, and mercy; these things by definition are *voluntary*. God could send us all to hell and remain holy, loving, and just.

By contrast, God's justice is inflexible. It is mandatory. Were he ever to relax his standards, he would cease to be God and the universe would implode. As John Stott has noted, "If God does not justly punish sin, he would be 'unjust to himself' . . . he would destroy both himself and us. He would cease to be God and we would cease to be fully human."[6] We can never fully know Christ as our lover until we first know him as judge, lawgiver, and king.

I say this for two important reasons.

First, God loves justice passionately. "I, the LORD, love justice" (Isa. 61:8). "The King is mighty, he loves justice" (Ps. 99:4). His justice is always according to holiness. It is precise, inflexible, and perfect. He rewards virtue according to its deserts and punishes every sin without favoritism and without exception. He "judges each man's work impartially" (1 Peter 1:17). And he judges according to divine righteousness. "God is a righteous judge" (Ps. 7:11).

God cannot compromise any virtue and remain holy, and this axiom applies especially to his justice. If he ever failed to punish a sin or to reward a virtuous act, he would be unrighteous, and God cannot be unrighteous. Therefore, he cannot forgive sin at the expense of justice. Sin must always be punished! Only after the satisfaction of the demands of justice can sin be forgiven. That is why Carnegie Simpson wrote, "Forgiveness is to man the plainest of duties; to God it is the profoundest of problems."[7]

Once anyone really sees the uncompromising nature of God's justice, the question is not why God finds it difficult to forgive sin, but how he finds it possible at all. How can God forgive sin and not compromise justice? J. I. Packer writes:

> God is not true to himself unless he punishes sin, and unless one knows and feels the truth of this fact, that wrongdoers have no natural hope of anything from God but retributive judgment, one can never share the biblical faith in divine grace.[8]

As we shall see, Paul's major premise in Romans 3:25–26 is that the cross proves emphatically that God loves justice.

A second proposition also follows. Wrath is God's righteous, or just, response to sin. "God's wrath in the Bible is always *judicial*—that is, it is the wrath of (a) Judge, administering justice."[9]

My point is that wrath is a virtue, not an evil. It is the righteous response to sin by a perfectly just Judge who loves virtue and hates evil. A God who does not visit sin with wrath cannot be good.

When my friend John said that his God was too good to express wrath, I responded, "The real problem is that your God is not good enough. How could any being that does not hate evil with an absolute hatred be good? A God that does not abhor evil and express wrath toward it would not be the holy, pure, and perfect God portrayed in the Bible."

"I'm not sure I buy that," John responded.

"Would a God who failed to judge Adolph Hitler be good?"

"Of course not," he answered.

"So you agree in principle that goodness cannot be apathetic to evil, that it must punish evil?"

"Well . . . yes . . . I see what you're driving at. I guess everyone believes that there is some behavior that is evil enough to merit God's anger," he conceded reluctantly.

"So then," I continued, "we must next decide if man is evil. If he is, goodness must declare itself with wrath. It must take sides. It cannot sit on the fence."

John walked away with a decision to make. Is man evil? Is God infinitely good? If so, the wrath of God must follow.

When it is all boiled down, our real problem with the wrath of God is pride. We don't really think we are evil, and we don't really think God is good. That is why A. W. Pink wrote, "Our readiness or our reluctance to meditate upon the wrath of God becomes a sure test of how our hearts really stand affected towards Him."[10]

The point is this: Wrath is the response of perfect goodness to wickedness and evil. We should rejoice in it. It is one great guarantee that God is absolutely good, and therefore trustworthy.

Another reason why we struggle with this concept is that we assume wrath is evil, and we know God cannot do evil. After all, human wrath is often evil. When a husband beats his wife in unrestrained fury, it is capricious, out of control, and a sign of self-centeredness. But God is "slow to anger" (Exod. 34:6). Wrath is his settled disposition to punish all evil according to the perfections of his inscrutable justice. It is controlled, deliberate, and always commensurate with the vice being punished. No one gets more or less wrath than he or she deserves.

In summary, God is absolutely just. Every sin must be and will be punished according to its deserts. There will be no exceptions.

God's Love for Sinners

Many Christians try to discuss the love of God without refer-ence to his justice and wrath, but this is at best inadequate, for the latter is the door into the experience of his infinite love. J. R. White writes, "God's love shines with its full and proper glory only when it is seen in its biblical context —against the backdrop of God's holiness and hatred of sin."[11] And John Stott adds, "The cross can be seen as proof of God's love only when it is at the same time seen as a proof of his justice."[12]

God longs to justify (declare "not guilty") sinners who justly deserve wrath. He passionately yearns to forgive and show them mercy. At the cross God accomplished both objectives. There he showed himself both "just [one who executes justice and always punishes sin] and the one who justifies [forgives and loves] those who have faith in Jesus" (Rom. 3:26).

The same moral perfection that provokes God's hatred of sin also prompts him to love the unlovable. God's goodness is like a coin with two faces. On one side is his hatred of evil, on the other his love of virtue. "For God so loved the world that he gave his one and only Son" (John 3:16). His love is an intense, omnipotent, tender yearning for the eternal happiness of crea-tures by nature at war with him, creatures who are cosmic rebels deserving only wrath. Because this love is so foreign to us, it needs clear definition.

When John writes, "God is love" (I John 4:16) he is not speaking primarily about affection. He is speaking about a holy love, one not common to this world. Therefore, affection did not primarily prompt God to send his Son. Rather, it was a love much deeper than affection—a deep, passionate longing for the happiness of those at war with him.

Jesus tells us, "Love your enemies and pray for those who per-secute you" (Matt. 5:44) because this is how God loved us. We are to "be perfect . . . as [our] heavenly Father is perfect" (Matt. 5:48). What makes God's love so holy and wonderful is that it is an outpouring of goodwill, at infinite expense for those who have sinned and turned away from him. Our fallen nature has no analogy for this kind of love. We might die for our friends, but never for our enemies.

God's love is also known by what it does. John 3:16 tells us that God loves the world, but I John 3:16 tells us *how* he loves it. "This is how we know what love is: Jesus Christ laid down his life for us." Love is known by its behavior, by its willingness to suffer for the happiness of the beloved. A young husband may kiss his wife and say, "I love you." But when he rises at 2:30 A.M. to rock a crying baby so that his wife can sleep, his behavior shouts his love. The old saying is true: Actions speak louder than words. And the cross trumpets God's infinite love in action.

It is difficult to understand the depth of this love because it is humanly impossible for us to comprehend the suffering of Christ, which is the heart of his actions. First, he descended an infinite distance from heaven to earth to take on human flesh. Since both we and our universe are finite, we can't imagine actions infinite in magnitude. We just take them by faith. But Jesus Christ left infinite joy and happiness to enter our fallen world. He lived in poverty and anonymity, suffered hunger, thirst, fatigue, insults, and rejection. Then he bore the sin of the universe on his shoulders and went to the cross.

Two aspects of this suffering especially magnify his love. First, Jesus bore human sin. Finite minds just aren't big enough to comprehend what it meant for Christ to be our sin bearer. I remember reading the story of a British officer captured by the Japanese in WWII. His captors wanted him to confess certain secrets, but they could not break his iron-willed, British discipline. So they searched for a personal weakness with which to break him. Finally, they discovered that he was fastidious. He hated filth. So they dug a pit, lowered him into it, and filled it up to his neck with human excrement. Within several days he became delirious, lost his mind, and told them everything. They broke him by immersing him in the one thing he most hated.

Sin is indescribably more offensive to God than human excrement was to that officer. The Old Covenant makes God's animosity agonizingly clear. "You hate all who do wrong" (Ps. 5:5). "There are six things the LORD hates, seven that are detestable to him" (Prov. 6:16). In fact, the word *detestable* (sometimes translated *abominable*) is used over one hundred times in the Old Testament alone to describe God's hatred of evil. To think that God willingly took sin upon himself—that which he hated with all the infinite intensity of omnipotence—is incomprehensible.

The second aspect of suffering was the Father's rejection. Most think that dread of this was what caused Jesus to sweat blood in the Garden of Gethsemane. The Father so hated sin that when his Son, the object of his infinite delight, bore our sin, he abandoned and rejected even him. "My God, my God, why have you forsaken me?" cried Jesus from the cross (Matt. 27:46). Remember, the Son of God was the apple of the Father's eye, the supreme object of his delight. The detestation of sin, and the love of God for you and me, had to be intense to motivate the Father to do this.

"I wish I had a deeper experience of the love of God," we complain. Well, look at the cross. That is where God's love is displayed. It appears nowhere else with such clarity. Meditate on it. Run to the glorious God revealed there. Put your trust in him. He is intensely interested in your eternal happiness. He will not abandon you. He will forgive and take to himself all who simply believe. His actions make this clear.

But it takes great humility to accept such love. I once witnessed to a woman deeply involved in a New Age religion. When I asked her how she would merit heaven, she responded, "I can't merit heaven now, but someday I will. I will be reincarnated many times, and each reincarnation will further purify me. Eventually, after many lives, I will be worthy of eternal life."

"I have good news," I said. "Just believe in Jesus and his work on the cross. He will clothe you in his righteousness. You will not need to be reincarnated. Your work will be over. Your sins will be forgiven, and you will be perfect in God's sight."

She gave me a stunned look. "That's too easy," she said with disbelief. "I am not taking a handout from God. I have my pride, you know."

"I know. That's the whole point. To have a relationship with God, you must die to your need to give something to God. Salvation is free. It is by grace. It is a gift from God."

My words were to no avail. She left convinced that she could be good enough, bound by her pride.

The Great Harmonizer

The cross synthesizes the wrath of God and the love of God. It satisfies both without compromising either. At the cross, the fear of God and the comfort of the Holy Spirit shake hands, the mercy of God and justice of God become friends. It is God's great harmonizer.

As Paul surveyed the Old Testament, he saw a problem. Romans 3:25–26 states God's solution. Let's read it again.

> He did this *to demonstrate his justice,* because in his forbearance he had left the sins committed beforehand unpunished—he did it to demonstrate his justice at the present time, so as to be *just and the one who justifies* those who have faith in Jesus.

> emphasis mine

Although God was just, many sinful saints (think of David and Bathsheba) had been forgiven and died with unpunished sins. How could perfect justice allow this? How could God justify sinners without first satisfying justice? To do so would be injustice, and God must be just.

The cross solves Paul's problem. There God punished all the sins of the Old Testament saints, who by faith were in Christ on the cross, with perfect justice. God's holy wrath was poured out upon them and his justice satisfied so that he could declare himself both just and the justifier of men like David.

God forgave David's adultery and murder on the basis of the cross. That is what Paul meant when he said "in his forbearance he had left the sins committed beforehand unpunished." As Dr. Denney has written,

> Christ's death, we may paraphrase (Paul's words in Romans 3:25), is an act in which God does justice to Himself. . . . He would not do justice to Himself if He displayed His compassion for sinners in a way which made light of sin, which ignored its tragic reality, or took it for less than it is. In this case He would again be doing Himself an injustice.[13]

In the same way God saves you and me—through faith in the cross of Christ—so that he can be both just and the lover of the unjust, punishing sin perfectly, glorifying both his love and justice in the redemption of sinful humankind.

The cross tells me everything I need to know about God. We have seen that the cross proclaims God's love for us and his passion for justice. The remainder of this chapter will examine what the cross says about God's delight in his law and his zeal for grace. We could discuss many other facts that the cross reveals about God, but because of space limitations we will content ourselves with these.

God's Passion for Law

Years ago I sold auto insurance to a man with two cars. He bought $25,000 underinsured motorist coverage on one car but $300,000 on the other. Several years later his wife was hit by an uninsured driver. She was in the car with the $25,000 limit, and she was paralyzed from the neck down. Her husband sued, claiming that he didn't know this car had lower limits.

I was asked to testify in the trial. I explained how the man had asked for the lower limit on the second car against my advice. I reminded the judge that before the accident the man had received approximately ten renewals showing the lower limits on this car, and that in an insurance review he had refused to raise the lower limits against my advice. I thought we had an airtight argument.

The judge ruled for the plaintiff, commanding us to extend the $300,000 limit to the car in question. I was shocked. What went wrong? The judge reminded us that although his verdict seemed unjust, there was a little-known state statute that commanded each insurer to notify all customers with different limits on their cars of this fact, and to be able to *prove* that they had done so in writing. We did not have this proof. I believe the judge wanted to rule in our favor, but he was passionately committed to upholding the law.

God is like this judge. He loves his law and will go to extremes to uphold it. When I first began to read Paul's epistles, I noticed Paul's statements about how the law, in some mysterious fashion, had been put aside. I rejoiced that law no longer mattered, that all that "legalism" was in the past. But when I began to understand the cross, I saw God's passion for law, and my perspective did an about-face.

The cross demonstrates the permanent, immutable nature of God's law. To save us, Jesus did not go around the law. He did not remove it. Rather, he fulfilled it. That is because the law is the eternal standard by which we will all be judged, and God is passionate about it. Every jot and tittle of the law must be fulfilled, promised Jesus (Matt. 5:17–20). The cross says, "There will be no lawbreakers in heaven." The cross says, "God is fervent about his law."

Verses such as "Now, by dying to what once bound us, we have been released from the law" (Rom. 7:6) have convinced many that law does not apply to Christians, that in some mysterious way it is no longer relevant or important. In one sense they are right. The law no longer enslaves Christians. We could not keep the law, so Jesus kept it for us. God has released all who put their trust in God's Son from the burden of being perfect law keepers. But the cross reminds us that we will never be released from the law as the standard for judgment.

Jesus did two things on our behalf to fulfill the law. First, he lived a perfect life. He obeyed every jot and tittle of the law so that he could impute that obedience to unworthy lawbreakers who put their faith in him. Second, on the cross he bore the punishment that lawbreakers deserve. Jesus glorified his Father's passion for his law by both fulfilling it and atoning for its abuse.

Behold God's passion for law! God would not save except by fulfilling and glorifying his law. The cross makes that clear. He paid an infinite price, the death of his Son, to uphold and glorify it, so it must matter greatly to him. With the cross in mind Paul wrote, "So then, the law is holy, and the commandment is holy, righteous and good" (Rom. 7:12). God has released us from the need to keep the law, not because the law is evil, unimportant, or irrelevant, but because Jesus kept it for us. It is the eternal standard that all must meet to enter God's holy place.

God's Zeal for Grace

Grace has many meanings in contemporary culture. It is usually a synonym for kindness. A gracious person is polite, kind, and defers to others. When we think of God's grace, we usually transfer this definition to him, but we impoverish ourselves greatly when we do so. Although we all sing the hymn "Amazing Grace," it amazes few. Why? Because grace cannot amaze until we feel the judgment we deserve.

The classic definition of grace is "unmerited favor." This definition is true, but it does not go deep enough. We comprehend grace when we see how unmerited God's favor is. Pink gives a better definition: "Grace then is favor shown where there is positive demerit in the one receiving it."[14]

To understand this definition we must contrast grace and mercy. Mercy reduces deserved punishment, but grace rewards those that deserve punishment. The difference between these two ideas is monumental.

For example, if a jury sentenced a serial murderer to death but the judge commuted the sentence to life in prison, the murderer would have received *mercy*, a reduction in punishment. Now pretend that the judge took the murderer's place in prison, gave him a million dollars as a gift, and sent him on an all-expenses-paid vacation to Hawaii, even while knowing the man was guilty. When someone who deserves punishment receives reward, he gets grace.

In God's eyes, you and I deserve capital punishment. We know this is true because the Father put Jesus to death in our place. Grace has no meaning apart from a clear understanding of what we deserve. The cross tells us all what we deserve—crucifixion—and only those with a clear view of the cross are amazed by grace.

This grace amazed John Newton. This is why he wrote the hymn "Amazing Grace." Newton became a Christian in his late twenties. Prior to his conversion, he had been a slave trader in West Africa and was a godless, ruthless man.

For example, he kept a black slave as a mistress. When he caught her in a sexual relationship with a black man, he beat the man to death with his shovel only to find out later that he was her husband.[15]

On the long voyages across the Atlantic, he and his mates raped the women being transported to their North American masters. Though many arrived pregnant with his seed, he was hard and indifferent to the fate of these women and their children.

That is why, after his conversion, Newton looked at the cross with amazement. There he saw grace—Christ suffering the agony of God's wrath in his place, so that God could reward him with eternal life. The grace of God stunned him, and he never got over it.

Our sins may be different from those of John Newton, but God's grace works the same way for us. When a Christian choral group changed the words in Newton's hymn from "saved a wretch like me" to "saved a person like me" I knew that grace had sprouted wings and flown away. Grace appears most perfectly in the knowledge of our sin revealed at the cross. Only cross-centered Christians find grace amazing.

Conclusion

How we think of God determines how we live and worship. The slow evolution of my understanding about God's nature has radically changed me.

When I saw that God loves his enemies, of which I was one, I began to love and forgive my enemies. When I saw the grace extended by God to me, I began to extend it to others. When I saw that God loved me from his will, rather than his feelings, I began to serve those that irritated me.

When I saw that Jesus died for me when I was an object of his wrath, I became secure in his love. If he died for me when I was morally reprehensible, I never need fear his rejection now that I am his friend. When I saw that God rewards sinners who deserve judgment, grace began to amaze me. If he loved me while I was a sinner, what will he withhold from me now that I am his friend? Answer? Nothing! (See Romans 8:32.)

At the cross, the love of God and the wrath of God shake hands; the mercy of God and the justice of God embrace; and the holiness of God and the sinfulness of humanity appear in stark contrast.

The cross teaches us to fear God and delight in his love at the same time. It makes us revel in the comfort of his awesome love while trembling in the presence of his glorious holiness. God is big, much bigger than any concept we now have of him; and we are small, much smaller than we have heretofore thought. And the cross is God's great pedagogue, eager to teach these life-transforming truths to all with eyes to see and ears to hear. Exult in the cross and behold God's glory (2 Cor. 3:17–18)!

4

The Worst of Sinners

The gospel tastes best to those who lie in the straits of death or whom an evil conscience oppresses, for in that case hunger is a good cook as we say, one who makes the food taste good. . . . But that hardened class who live in their own holiness, build on their own works, and feel not their sin and misery do not taste this food. Whoever sits at a table and is hungry relishes all, however, he who is sated relishes nothing.

Martin Luther

King David asked, "What is man that you are mindful of him?" (Ps. 8:4). He was puzzled that God would notice or love anyone as perverse and corrupt as he was. God's extravagant grace constantly amazed him.

Paul saw himself in a similar light. At the end of his life, after all of his amazing revelations and his Herculean, mind-stupefying sufferings to extend God's kingdom, all he could say of himself was "Christ Jesus came into the world to save sinners—*of whom I am the worst"* (I Tim. 1:15, emphasis mine). Imagine, Paul, the worst of sinners? Surely, compared to you and me, he was the greatest of saints. Was Paul exaggerating, or did he see himself accurately? I contend that Paul, as do all who really know God, saw himself accurately *because* he saw himself in the light of the cross.

A Christian friend recently shared a frustration. The longer he related to Christ, the more incompetent and unworthy he felt. He assumed that something was wrong, that his experience should be just the opposite, that maturity would bring a feeling of having it more together.

"Your experience is normal," I reassured him. "The closer you draw to Christ, the more clearly you will see yourself. You will see your sin more clearly, abhor it more perfectly, feel less confidence in yourself, be more dependent upon Christ, and feel more loved by God. As this process advances, you will need God more, depend upon him increasingly, and become more effective for Christ and his kingdom."

Although my friend listened sincerely, I'm not sure he understood what I was saying. My advice merely summed up the experience of God's greatest servants. As J. C. Ryle notes,

> I am persuaded that the more light we have, the more we see our own sinfulness; the nearer we get to heaven, the more we are clothed with humility. In every age of the church you will find it true, if you will study biographies, that the most eminent saints—men like Bradford, Rutherford and McCheyne—have always been the humblest men.[1]

But this is not what today's Christian expects. Contemporary psychology and popular self-help theories have seduced us. We have bought the lie that we have dignity because we are good.

By contrast, the Bible tells us that we have dignity despite the complete *absence* of any saving virtue. If Christianity is true, then the cross of Christ is the only ground for human dignity. Paul expressed this dependence well. "May I never boast except in the cross of our Lord Jesus Christ" (Gal. 6:14). The cross, not our inherent goodness, is the Christian's only grounds for dignity.

Men are proud. Nothing stirs up conflict quicker than a sermon on human bankruptcy, moral wickedness, and perversity. Yet the Bible consistently testifies that God sees us precisely in this way. Paul wrote the first three chapters of Romans, his magnum opus, to make this point.

Three is God's number of exclamation, and three times the Bible states, "There is no one who does good, not even one" (Rom. 3:12; Ps. 14:3; Ps. 53:3). And for emphasis, Paul added, "All have sinned and fall short of the glory of God" (Rom. 3:23).

So David's question remains: "What is man that you are mindful of him?" Are we basically good or basically evil? Does God love us because of our goodness or despite its complete absence?

Too Much or Too Little Esteem?

The cross, and the context of the Bible, repeatedly speak to us about our systemic evil. We are arrogant, and this pride is the source of most human grief. These facts collide with today's worldview. *World* magazine columnist Elizabeth Nickson has noted that the word *self-esteem* appears in the titles of at least three thousand contemporary books.[2] Our culture assumes that we have too little self-esteem (read "pride") and that this lack explains everything from poor junior high test scores to burglary and rape. God's perspective differs radically. Self-exaltation, not poor self-esteem, destroys human achievement and happiness.

So is our esteem too low or too high? We don't even need to go to the Bible to end this debate. The discipline of social psychology has already answered it conclusively.

In his perceptive book *The Inflated Self,* David Myers sums up a lot of research. For example:

Jean-Paul Codol conducted twenty experiments with French people ranging from twelve-year-old school children to adult professionals. Regardless of those involved and the experimental methods, the people's self-perceived superiority was present consistently. . . . People saw themselves as more *cooperative* than others; if given a competitive task, they perceived themselves as more *competitive* than others. Codol also found that the more people admired a particular trait, the more likely they were to see this trait as truer of themselves than of others.[3]

emphasis mine

In a survey by *U.S. News and World Report*,[4] Americans were asked whom they thought most likely to go to heaven. Sixty-five percent thought Oprah Winfrey and Michael Jordan were "very likely" to go to heaven. Seventy-nine percent believed Mother Teresa would go to heaven. There was only one person who scored higher than Mother Teresa. You guessed it—the respondent. Over 80 percent taking the survey felt they were "very likely" to go to heaven. Our problem is a profound feeling of false innocence, hidden behind the blindness of high self-esteem (the Bible calls it pride). The church labors under the same delusion.

In the fall of 2001 George Barna polled six hundred senior pastors of Protestant churches in the United States. He asked them to rate their job performance on eleven distinct pastoral functions ranging from preaching to fund-raising. Obviously, 50 percent of these pastors are average or above average in each category and 50 percent average or below average.

They were asked to score themselves excellent, good, average, not too good, and poor. What were the results? Ninety-five percent rated their preaching average or above average. Eighty-seven percent rated their leadership skills average or above average. As a group, they rated themselves lowest in fund-raising. Only 59 percent rated their fund-raising abilities average or above average.[5]

In every job category, well over 50 percent rated themselves average or above average. And in ten of the eleven categories, less than 10 percent rated themselves in the not too good or poor categories. In four job categories, less than 2 percent rated themselves below average. Don't you wish this described our pastors? Like their secular counterparts, our spiritual leaders have an inflated self-perception, very unlike their heroes, men like Job, Isaiah, or Paul.

Sometimes people do feel inferior to their peers. But Dr. Myers notes that it tends to be in the presence of a superior *individual*, one who is better looking, smarter, better educated, or wealthier. The other exception occurs in clinically depressed people who also view themselves realistically. But when comparing ourselves to the norms of society, most of us feel above average.

In fact, this arrogance is so prominent in social research that many social scientists have concluded that evolution has built a significant load of unreality into us for survival. In summary, these experiments confirm what the Bible has taught for four thousand years: Pride, not low self-esteem, is our basic problem.[6]

Please note, I am not saying that guilt is not a pervasive problem. It is. What I am saying is that pride is an even greater problem. Moreover, I am convinced that pride—too high of an opinion of oneself—rather than low self-esteem, causes most guilt. It is the root that feeds most self-hatred. We feel that we are capable of high-level moral performance. When we fail, that assumption fuels most self-hatred and guilt. But the humble understand their weak impotence. They have no illusions about themselves. "Apart from me you can do nothing" (John 15:5), is constantly in their thinking. They struggle less with guilt as they grow progressively humble. A profound, God-sent humility is the cure for most self-hatred.

Biblical Testimony

Scripture never encourages us to think more highly of ourselves. The Bible does not assume that low self-esteem is our problem. The omniscient Holy Spirit, who understands us perfectly, knows both our problem and its cure. The Bible preaches that too much, not too little, self-esteem is the problem for most of us.

Instead, the Bible abounds with statements like "Humble yourselves before the Lord" (James 4:10). And "Clothe yourselves with humility toward one another, because, 'God opposes the proud but gives grace to the humble'" (1 Peter 5:5). Scripture also says to "not think of yourself more highly than you ought, but rather think of yourself with sober judgment" (Rom. 12:3). Why? Because we constantly think more highly of ourselves than we should.

God knows that we are naturally conceited. Therefore, he commands us, "Do not be proud, but be willing to associate with people of low position. Do not be conceited" (Rom. 12:16).

Because we naturally consider ourselves more important than others, Paul urges us, "Do nothing out of selfish ambition or vain conceit, but in humility consider others better than yourselves" (Phil. 2:3).

A New Perspective Is Needed

We cure arrogance by looking at God. We cannot see ourselves correctly by comparing ourselves to others. We do not become humble by scrutinizing ourselves under a microscope of guilt. Rather, we must see ourselves with God's eyes, in God's light. We need a heavenly perspective to become humble. The bigger God gets, the smaller and more humble we feel.

We feel this humility when we survey the vastness of the starry universe on a summer night, or when we view the earth turning slowly under a satellite cam on TV. In both cases we see ourselves from a new perspective by looking outward. As Winston Churchill (probably not a Christian) aptly observed, "We are only specks of dust that have settled in the night on the map of the world."

The dark night, bejeweled with stars in glorious array, is big, but it is finite. It has an end. But the God who spoke it into existence is *infinite* in size, power, and most importantly, moral holiness. We cannot see ourselves aright when humanity is our only point of reference. We must see ourselves through God's eyes, comparing ourselves to the holy whiteness of his moral purity. No one who has seen himself or herself in God's light can remain arrogant.

The heroes of the Bible became humble in this way. Job was "blameless and upright; he feared God and shunned evil" (Job 1:1). But when this "good" man saw himself in God's light he said, "I *despise myself* and repent in dust and ashes" (Job 42:6, emphasis mine).

When Isaiah encountered Jehovah high and lifted up, he groaned, "Woe to me! . . . *I am ruined!* For I am a man of unclean lips" (Isa. 6:5, emphasis mine). What happened to these godly men? They saw themselves in God's light, in stark contrast to him, and they became humble. We are no different today.

I remember the story of a small group's prayer meeting. They enjoyed profound fellowship with God and one another. Then an uninvited member of the congregation joined. He was a proud, religious man, and his presence grieved God's Spirit. When he came, the sweetness of God's presence left. So the group prayed, "God, please bring our friend to real repentance so that we can once again enjoy your presence."

At their next meeting, God's presence returned. Only this time the uninvited guest also sensed God's presence for the first time. God revealed himself as the Holy One to this man. The man saw himself as God saw him. He began to cough and gag. Then he threw himself face down on the floor. With profuse weeping he began to confess horrible, secret sins in graphic detail. The light of God banished his proud, religious spirit.

You don't need to have this kind of experience to be humbled. You merely need to see God and self at the foot of the cross, because the cross profoundly humbles everyone who understands its message. For there we see God, dying for his enemies. "When we were God's enemies, we were reconciled to him through the death of his Son" (Rom. 5:10). This is the perspective that gives us God's self-esteem. To obtain this we need to see the nature of the enmity between us and God.

According to *Webster's Dictionary* an enemy is "a person who hates, opposes, or fosters harmful designs against another; a hostile opponent." The enmity between God and man is profound. The cross reveals it, and it cuts two ways. God is alienated from us, and we are estranged from him. The cross speaks four crucial truths about this enmity:

1. Unredeemed humans are objects of God's wrath.
2. Unredeemed humans actually hate God.
3. Unredeemed humans are morally bankrupt.
4. The cross of Christ is the only valid ground for human dignity.

Objects of Wrath

God's love is more than a feeling. It is a decision to live for the happiness of another. Some define it as a decision for another's happiness even at your expense. "Agape love is not primarily an emotion," writes Paul Billheimer, "but aggressive, benevolent, sacrificial, outgoing goodwill. It is the soul of ethics."[7] This is how God loves us. He longs for our happiness with all the intensity of divine jealousy and all the power of omnipotence, even while, in our unredeemed state, we are "by nature objects of wrath" (Eph. 2:3).

Wrath implies enmity, and we just read Webster's definition. Leon Morris points out that there are over 580 references to God's wrath toward fallen man in the Old Testament alone.[8] The New Testament repeatedly builds on this truth. Jesus died for the wicked (Rom. 4:5), the enemies of God (Rom. 5:10), those hostile to him, those at enmity with him (Col. 1:21), and those by "nature objects of wrath" (Eph. 2:3).

The cross enables us to understand this idea. The nature of the atonement displays God's animosity toward fallen man. Jesus stood in as our substitute on the cross. He took our sins upon himself. Then the Father gave him what we, and our sins, deserve. He crucified him and rejected him. He treated him as a dreaded enemy. He forsook him. "My God, my God, why have you forsaken me?" agonized Christ (Matt. 27:46). At the cross God struck his beloved Son with the wrath that you and I deserve.

The cross graphically reveals what the wrath of God looks like. Jesus was mocked because we deserve to be mocked (Prov. 1:26–27). He was stripped and beaten because we deserve the same. He was crowned with thorns because we deserve to be crowned with thorns. He was rejected because we deserve to be rejected. The authorities nailed him to the cross and slowly tortured him to death because we deserve to be nailed and tortured in the same way. Crucifixion is what sin and sinners deserve.

This is a sobering message. In fact, the cross is the ultimate demonstration of God's wrath, so prominent throughout the Old Testament. All 580 references to God's wrath in the Old Testament point to this one poignant moment in human history, the moment when God's beloved Son would drink the wine of the fury of the wrath of God Almighty in order to secure the happiness of his enemies (Rev. 16:19).

The subtleties of twenty-first-century thinking have not changed this reality. Secular North America is alienated from God. In his sight we are a "corrupt generation" (Acts 2:40) and "the wrath of God is being revealed from heaven" against us (Rom. 1:18).

This truth is distressing. It deflates our arrogance. It humbles us in the dust. It is hard to receive. But our reaction to this truth, and our propensity to pride, is not new. It is our eternal condition. In the seventeenth century Blaise Pascal cautioned that it is as equally dangerous for man to know God without knowing his own sinfulness as it is for him to know about his sinfulness without knowing the Redeemer who can cure him.[9]

Pascal's first concern, knowing God without knowing our sinfulness, is today's great problem. Because most Christians do not understand the cross, they think too well of themselves. But it was at the cross where God publicly displayed his hostility to sin and sinners. At the cross we come to grips with our sinfulness so that we can later fall in love with God and revel in his infinite love.

In summary, although sin alienates God from man, God has used our rebellion for good. The animosity of God toward both sin and sinners, as we shall see, ends up displaying the glory and majesty of his love in a way that could not have occurred without this profound alienation.

▄▄ *Hatred of God*

The cross teaches us that fallen man hates God. "If the world hates you," Jesus warned his disciples, "keep in mind that it hated me first" (John 15:18). By "the world" Jesus meant all those outside of him. Unredeemed men are by nature God-haters. Examine the biblical evidence with me and see if this conclusion isn't right.

"My unbelieving friends don't hate God," you may object. "They are good people. They would love God if they just had enough faith to believe in him."

I agree that everyone loves the *image* of God that they have fabricated in their own thinking. "My God would never do that.

He is a loving God," people often say. But the expression "my God" says it all. He is not the just, holy God who has objectively revealed himself in the Bible and who died on the cross to forgive us and separate us from our sins. He is not the glorious God who hates sin, and judges sinners with wrath. He is a subjective god of our own imagination.

If you don't believe this proposition, when you're at a party, bring up the subjects of hell, the wrath of God, God's hatred of sin, or the judgment to come, and watch the reaction.

Remember, Jesus said, "Everyone who does evil hates the light, and will not come into the light for fear that his deeds will be exposed" (John 3:20). Jesus spoke of himself. He is the light of the world. We have all been light-haters at one time and were therefore, by definition, haters of Jesus Christ.

Still not convinced? Look at the cross. When God incarnated himself in human flesh and came to live among his chosen people, the Jewish nation, those who claimed to love and follow him, what did they do? They exchanged the God of glory, whom they claimed to love and worship, for Barabbas, a common criminal, and sent their Lord to a brutal, horrible death. They hated him!

It is this message, what the cross says about man, that makes it, in Paul's terms, "offensive" (Gal. 5:11), a "stumbling stone" (Rom. 9:32), the "smell of death" (2 Cor. 2:16), and "foolishness" (1 Cor. 1:18) to the unbelieving mind. John Piper notes,

> God's wisdom exalts what the cross stands for, and human wisdom is offended by what the cross stands for. What does it stand for? The cross stands for the ungodliness and helplessness of man (Rom. 5:6), the glorious grace of God (Rom. 3:24), and the unimpeachable justice of God (Rom. 3:25, 26).[10]

In fact, it is what the cross says about God and man that caused most of Paul's vast persecutions.[11] This is why Paul came fearfully to Corinth. "For I resolved to know nothing while I was with you except Jesus Christ and him crucified. I came to you in weakness and fear, and with much trembling" (I Cor. 2:2–3).

Paul came in weakness, fear, and much trembling because he feared the persecution that usually followed the cross message about man and God. On the other hand, those who preach Paul's message will also get Paul's results. This is the message that provokes God to release his power to crush stony hearts, bringing them into his kingdom. That is why Paul says in the next verse: "My message and my preaching were . . . with a demonstration of the Spirit's power" (I Cor. 2:4).

The great nineteenth-century Scottish theologian, George Smeaton, observed: "For God inhabits that word which is based on the incarnation and the cross. It is the habitation of His power—it is, as it were, His chariot; all the attributes of God surround it and adorn it (Heb. 4:12); but let anything else be substituted for the cross, and preaching is denuded of its efficacy, and stripped of its power."[12] The cross reminds us that unredeemed man hates God. This is a difficult message. Don't shrink from it. It is crucial to the release of God's power.

Moral Bankruptcy

The cross also speaks to us about our moral bankruptcy. If we could have earned God's favor, the cross would not have been necessary. The cross says, "The river of sin is so wide that none can ford it. God had to build a bridge." All human effort to find peace with God is in vain.

There is nothing we can do but believe and repent, and because of the cross this is enough. We are beggars for mercy, and God delights to have it that way "so that no one can boast" (Eph. 2:9). Humble people are happy, and the cross humbles us into true happiness.

One morning a friend asked how I was doing. "It's a bad day. I'm depressed. I just took a new job, and I think I made a mistake,"

I replied. Compassionately he took my wife and me to dinner that night, and we had a wonderful time. When he insisted on picking up the dinner tab it took all my self-control to let him serve us so extravagantly. I felt indebted to his kindness, and I wanted to repay him.

We feel the same way toward God, but we cannot repay or earn his kindness. We must just humble ourselves and receive free, unearnable, and unmerited grace. The cross makes this clear. As John Stott observes:

> As we stand before the cross, we begin to gain a clear view both of God and of ourselves, especially in relation to each other . . . we cannot bear to acknowledge either the seriousness of our sin and guilt or our utter indebtedness to the cross. . . . This is the scandal, the great stumbling block, of the cross. For our proud hearts rebel against it. . . . Surely, we say, there must be something we can do, or at least contribute, in order to make amends?[13]

Here also is the great divide, the great chasm, separating Christianity from every other religion. The cross proclaims our utter helplessness and bankruptcy. It says, "The righteous will live by faith" (Rom. 1:17), not by their hard work.

By contrast, every other world religion practices some form of self-help. "I will be good enough. I will not enter a relationship to which I cannot contribute, even with God," says the proud heart. Either through the cycles of reincarnation, obedience to the laws of Moses, faithfulness to the Koran, or ages of suffering in purgatory, man intends to "earn" a place in God's presence and therefore have something of which to boast.

But the cross says, "Impossible!" Man and God are at war. God requires perfection, and no man can be perfect. Therefore, God became perfect for us. He saves those who believe, who humble themselves, who become debtors to his rich mercy and express their gratitude with a life of joyful, repentant obedience.

■ *Human Dignity*

A person with dignity conducts himself or herself in a way that displays their self-respect. The cross speaks to us about the only biblical basis for human dignity—and what an amazing basis it is. Despite our vast sin our souls are precious in his sight.

Yes, we have dignity, not because we are good, but despite the fact that we are not. The death of Christ crowns us with dignity. It says, "You have value, but only because I love you. And I have loved you despite the vast enmity that stands between us." Such wondrous love is incomprehensible.

In fact, God loves us passionately, and the wonder of God's love is that he lavishes it upon his enemies. The cross makes the glorious nature of this love very clear. George Smeaton writes: "The death of Christ, far transcending every example of human love, which hardly ever dreamt of laying down one's life for a friend, was a display of love for enemies."[14]

A mother will arise at 2 A.M. to nurse and rock the baby for which she feels great affection. A father will spend large sums of money on his child's college education. But God crucified his Son to lavish infinite happiness on enemies. We have no way to compute this, because no one reading this would ever make these sacrifices for an enemy, let alone die for one. In fact, very few of us would die for a friend.

I remember reading about a Vietnam-era soldier who threw himself on an enemy hand grenade to save his buddies. This kind of self-sacrifice amazes us, and it should. This man gave his life for his friends, but at the cross God threw himself on a grenade to save the enemy soldiers on the other side of the sandbags—men intent on destroying him. Do you see it, the matchless love of God? And our unworthiness only magnifies it.

Not only did God die for his enemies, but he also died for enemies he did not need. If God lacked happiness he would not be the complete and perfect God revealed in Scripture. We can give God nothing. Our redemption does not fulfill a need in God. "Who has ever given to God, that God should repay him?" (Rom. 11:35). Answer? No one!

Then why did Christ die for us? That is the great question for which no satisfactory answer exists—except God's overflowing love, goodwill, and all-consuming passion for the happiness of his undeserving creatures. In the last analysis, this is the only ground for human dignity.

In summary, the cross displays the glory and wonder of God's love only to the degree that we see our unworthiness of that love and our inability to give him anything. With all this in mind J. I. Packer wrote:

It is staggering that God should love sinners; yet it is true. God loves creatures who have become unlovely and (one would have thought) unlovable. There was nothing whatever in the objects of his love to call it forth; nothing in us could attract or prompt it. Love among persons is awakened by something in the beloved, but the love of God is free, spontaneous, unevoked, uncaused. God loves people because he has chosen to love them—as Charles Wesley put it, "he hath loved us, he hath loved us, because he would love" (an echo of Deut. 7: 7–8)—and no reason for his love can be given except his own sovereign good pleasure.[15]

We see the reflection of his infinite love in the mirror of our lowliness and sinfulness. We see our sinfulness at the cross. When we do, we worship him for the beauty of his holiness. We rejoice in a glorious dignity that is grounded in God's decision to love the unlovable.

Conclusion

Let me conclude with four important observations.

First, God designed our salvation to glorify himself and humble us. "The eye of the arrogant man will be humbled and the pride of men brought low; the LORD alone will be exalted in that day" (Isa. 2:11). "That day" was the day of Christ's crucifixion.

Second, you can expect nothing from the world but hostility to this message. You cannot be used by God to reach others unless you are willing to be hated by them, because fallen humankind does not like what the cross says about people. Jesus warned: "If the world hates you, keep in mind that it hated me first" (John 15:18). The power of God is in the proclamation of the cross and all that it teaches about God and humanity. If you are loved by all people, it could be that something is wrong with your message.

Paul expected the gospel to divide. He knew that it produced no middle ground. It was either the stench of death or the fragrance of life to those who heard. "For we are to God the aroma of Christ among those who are being saved and those who are perishing. To the one we are the smell of death; to the other, the fragrance of life. And who is equal to such a task?" (2 Cor. 2:15–16).

Paul built churches upon those to whom the cross was a "fragrance of life." Those to whom it was "the smell of death" persecuted him bitterly. It was not what the cross declared about God's love that caused this persecution. It was what it said about God's holiness, justice, wrath, and man's sinful impotence. Because of this message, Paul bore on his "body the marks of Jesus" (Gal. 6:17).

Third, the great irony is that the door through which we experience the profundity of God's love is the complete humiliation and abasement of ourselves at the foot of the cross. Jesus promised, "Blessed are the poor in spirit, for theirs is the kingdom of heaven" (Matt. 5:3). The blessing of knowing God in the fullness of his love comes to us to the degree that we become poor in Spirit. This glorious spiritual destitution belongs to those who hear what the cross teaches us about man and his nature.

"What is man that you are mindful of him?" asked David (Ps. 8:4). The cross answers, "He is nothing in himself. He is everything because God loves him, and God demonstrated that love at the cross." May God wash us all in the joy of this reality.

Fourth, God will crown your ministry with success if you boldly proclaim the cross. In God's kingdom, the way up is the way down. If we are ever to be truly helpful, we must begin with our sin and all it means. To disseminate the fragrance of God's love, we must help others see themselves before the cross of Christ "wretched, pitiful, poor, blind and naked" (Rev. 3:17). The cross is God's mirror. There we behold ourselves as we really are. Gaze into it daily.

5

For God's Glory

God had a design of glorifying himself from eternity, yea,
to glorify each person in the Godhead . . . and the principal
mean that he adopted was this great work of redemption.
It was his design in this work to glorify his only-begotten
Son, Jesus Christ; and by the Son to glorify the Father.

Jonathan Edwards

In my early twenties I worked for a small business. The owner
and all his employees were Christians. We were very idealistic.
We prayed together every morning. We prayed for our customers. We even gave them free merchandise if we thought they were
needy. We assumed that all we had to do was take care of people,
and profit would take care of itself. We served customers, ignored
profit, and went out of business.

A few months later I went to work for a small contractor.
He was not a Christian. He was greedy. Nothing mattered but
profit. He abused his employees and cheated his customers. His
crew, including myself, eventually quit and took other jobs. His

dissatisfied customers went elsewhere. He was also soon out of business.

Both of these businesses failed because they lost sight of the proper *end* of business and the *means* to get there. They did not pursue the right end with the best means. Profit is the proper *end* of business: It is the reason businesses exist. Serving customers and employees are the proper *means* to that objective. My first employer made the means the end. My second employer pursued the right end with a perverse means. Both failed.

The church is similar. The *end* of the church is the glory of God. "In the Ultimate Sense," notes Millard Erickson, "the purpose of God's plan is His glory. This is the highest of all values, and the one great motivating factor in all that God has chosen and done."[1] Loving God and people are *means* to that end. When we make the means (people) the end, or pursue the glory of God with a carnal means, the church slowly goes out of business.

For the most part, the church is ignorant of God's ultimate end for its existence. "Many churches . . . have degenerated into self-serving enterprises whose primary celebration is to exalt God as giver and the validation of a message of cultural narcissism and personal advantages," notes John Hannah, professor at Dallas Theological Seminary. "Such churches have accommodated themselves to things that are not eternal."[2]

Many of us are like the athlete who purchased athletic shoes before she knew what sport she was going to play, or like the computer engineer designing a complex microprocessor with absolutely no idea why he is building it. In short, like my first employer who served people but ignored profit, we suffer. In a spiritual sense, without a clear understanding of God's end and why we exist, we fail at the business of serving God.

Our goal is not the happiness of people, or even self-fulfillment. Our goal is to give glory to God. This is the reason God created and redeemed us.

Jesus, Our Model

By definition Christians are followers and imitators of Christ. We are duty-bound to think and live as he did. This includes discovering and adopting Christ's end for life. And his purpose was no mystery.

The glory of God was always Jesus' first ambition. He consistently subordinated the happiness and welfare of people to this one overriding objective. When he loved people it was for his Father's sake, and then for their sake. We are saved precisely because Jesus sought his Father's glory above all else. The same principle applies to the church. We become helpful to this world to the degree that we die to it and live for the glory of God.

I am not minimizing his love for us. The human mind cannot comprehend the love of God (Eph. 3:18–19). It overwhelms all who experience it. I am just saying that he loved the glory of his Father more.

Jesus was transparent about his mission. He lived to please his Father. "I always do what pleases him" (John 8:29). "I tell you the truth, the Son can do nothing by himself; he can do only what he sees his Father doing, because whatever the Father does the Son also does" (John 5:19). "I have brought you glory on earth by completing the work you gave me to do" (John 17:4).

A Cross for God's Glory

Jesus' actions and statements in the last week of his life—as he approached his cross—best reveal the radical nature of his purpose.

First century Judeans were poverty stricken. The destitution of the average Israelite was well below that of today's lowest welfare recipient. Often, they had food only for that day, and many went hungry. That is why, after Jesus multiplied bread and fish in John

75

chapter 6, the crowds tried to make him king by force. His en-thronement meant daily bread.

A few days before Jesus' death, Simon the Leper invited him to a feast. At Simon's banquet Mary opened a bottle of perfume and poured it over Jesus' feet and head. The perfume was worth a year's wages, about thirty thousand dollars in today's money—enough money to feed many hungry children of God.

Judas was upset. "Why wasn't this perfume sold and the money given to the poor?" (You and I probably would have asked the same question.)

Jesus' answer is not what we expect. "Leave her alone. It was intended that she should save this perfume for the day of my burial. You will always have the poor among you, but you will not always have me."

Let me take the liberty to amplify Jesus' answer in my own words. "The Father has intended that this expensive bottle of perfume be lavished on me rather than the poor. The will of the Father is more important than all the suffering of the poor combined. Mary has recognized this and done right. Mary thinks as I do; she is radically Father-centered. She perceives that my death and burial are for God's glory, and she has done the one thing that matters."

This statement would be ugly arrogance from any of us. But Jesus was God, the Maker of the universe. "The LORD works out everything for his own ends" (Prov. 16:4), including money that could have fed the poor.

Then a few hours later, with the burden of his death pressing upon him, Jesus prayed, "Now my heart is troubled, and what shall I say? 'Father, save me from this hour'? No, it was for this very reason that I came to this hour. *Father, glorify your name!*" (John 12:27–28, emphasis mine).

He abhorred the cross. He trembled at the thought of its suf-fering and shame, but he was determined to endure it because he knew it would glorify his Father. (Our happiness and redemption were an important secondary motivation.)

The cross glorified God while at the same time securing the redemption of sinners. It displayed forever, for all to see, the moral glory, the incomprehensible goodness, of the God who created all things. As we saw in the last chapter, the cross put on display God's passion for justice, his unfathomable love of unworthy sinners, his amazing grace, his passion for law, his hatred of sin, and the glory of his just wrath, deservingly poured out on evil. To display this for his Father's satisfaction was Jesus' first reason for existence. "For this very reason I came to this hour. Father, glorify your name" (John 12:27–28).

Jesus' prayer life speaks to this thesis. If you knew you were going to die in a few hours and had one last chance to pray, you probably would intercede about the few things in life that really mattered. It might be the welfare of your family or maybe the forgiveness of your sin. Faced with this predicament, Jesus prayed, "Father, the time has come. Glorify your Son, that your Son may glorify you" (John 17:1). He focused on glorifying his Father—even if it meant death on a cross. As Daniel Fuller notes,

> His motive in dying for us was not to restore our ruined reputation but to uphold the great worth of God's glory. Jesus' stated concern in dying for sinners was to glorify the Father by showing that His goodness, culminating in His display of mercy, was valuable enough to die for.[3]

Glory: God's Eternal End

For eternity God has delighted, above all else, in his glory.[4] Before mass, space, and time existed, God fellowshipped in a Trinity of infinite love. In what did he love and delight? Each member of the Godhead exulted in the perfections of the moral beauty—love, grace, righteousness, justice, etc.—that they beheld in each other. This love boiled over in an infinite ocean of joy and pleasure.[5] The Bible refers to this moral beauty as the glory of God. It is a term for the perfections and splendor of his personality expressed by his divine attributes.

When God decided to create the universe, he did so to perpetuate, display, and enhance this delight in himself. He created to display his glory. "Bring My sons from afar and My daughters from the ends of the earth, everyone who is called by My name, and whom I have created for My glory" (Isa. 43:6–7 NASB). He also redeems to display his glory.

> Therefore say to the house of Israel, "This is what the Sovereign Lord says: It is not for your sake, O house of Israel, that I am going to do these things [give you a New Covenant and redemption], but for the sake of my holy name, which you have profaned among the nations where you have gone. I will show the holiness of my great name, which has been profaned among the nations, the name you have profaned among them. Then the nations will know that I am the Lord, declares the Sovereign Lord, when I show myself holy through you before their eyes."[6]
>
> Ezekiel 36:22–23

God's first motive is not our welfare. It is his name, which is his glory. After an exhaustive study of the biblical evidence, Jonathan Edwards concluded, "On the whole, I think it is pretty manifest, that Jesus Christ sought the glory of God as his highest and last end; and that therefore . . . this was God's last end in the creation of this world."[7]

Fallen Short of His Glory

My three-year-old grandson loves to put on a show for his extended family. When he does, we laugh and applaud. He thinks he is the center of the world, but I don't get too upset about that. He has good parents. I know he will outgrow his self-centeredness. If he didn't, he would become a monster.

In the same way, God intends the normal process of spiritual maturation to move us from self-centeredness to a life consumed with passion for his glory, the purpose for our existence. But our fallen nature often resists this transformation.

Even after conversion to a God-glorifying life, we find in our flesh all kinds of selfish motives. Just about the time I gain some small victory over the lust for self-glorification, I find new self-oriented desires sprouting up in some hidden corner of my heart. And I am not alone in this.

I arrived at a Christian worker's conference scheduled to do four workshops. At the general session that began the meetings, the master of ceremonies called one of the other workshop leaders onto the stage. He told the audience that this man's videos were national best-sellers, that he was a tremendous speaker, and that everyone should attend his workshop.

I looked at my schedule. His workshop was at the same time as mine. My heart fell. *No one will come to my session,* I thought. I resented the MC, envied the other speaker, and felt ridiculous for having wasted my time on this conference.

The problem was simple: I wanted the glory! I anxiously fretted over my predicament for several minutes. Although I looked spiritual on the outside, I was self-seeking on the inside and unintentionally resisting God's plan.

Then the Holy Spirit reminded me of John the Baptist's eight powerful words: "He must become greater; I must become less" (John 3:30). Right away, I saw my sin in God's light. *God,* I prayed, *work through his workshop and send people to his meeting if necessary. Glorify yourself through his ministry.* God's joy and peace quickly drove away the resentment and jealousy I had been nursing.

Paul wrote, "All have sinned and fall short of the glory of God" (Rom. 3:23). To live for any purpose except the glory of God is to fall short of his glory. "[We] tend to think of God and the whole Christian salvation as something to solve our problems," notes Dr. Martyn Lloyd-Jones. But, he writes,

> the whole purpose of your salvation and mine is that we should glorify the Father. . . . The essence of sin is not to glorify God, and anybody who does not glorify God is guilty of sin of the foulest kind. Even though you may never have got drunk, though you may never be guilty of adultery, if you live for yourself and your own glory you are as desperate a sinner as those other people whom you regard as sinners.[8]

If you moved to the slums of Calcutta and exhausted your time and wealth to serve the poor but did it for no other motive than love of the poor, it would not be virtue from God's perspective. It would be sin. It might earn the praise of men, but because it was done for the happiness of people as its first end, rather than for the glory of God, it would only enhance your judgment from God. It is idolatry to serve others without reference to the glory of God.

God's Solution

God has provided two glorious solutions for our waywardness. First, Jesus did everything for the glory of God; he entertained no lesser motives. When you and I trust in him for salvation, God imputes his motives (his passion for his Father's glory) to us, declaring us not guilty of falling short of the glory of God.[9]

Second, at our New Birth, God gives us a growing zeal to live for his glory. Regeneration, among other things, is an infusion of God's very life, and that life is passionate for God's glory. Remember, this has been his aim and obsession for eternity. Since New Birth is a share in God's nature, by definition it must bring a growing ardor for the same purpose. If we claim to have the Holy Spirit but have no growing passion for the Father's glory, we are self-deceived.

God called David Morgan to preach the gospel during the 1859 Welsh Revival. On New Year's Day he conducted a meeting at the Devil's Bridge. A fellow minister described the night.

> The evening service was terrible. So near was the revivalist to his God, that his face shone like that of an angel, so that none could gaze steadfastly at him. Many of the hearers swooned. On the way home I dared not break the silence for miles. Towards midnight I ventured to say, "Didn't we have blessed meetings, Mr. Morgan?"
>
> "Yes," he replied, and after a pause, added, "The Lord would give us great things, if He could only trust us."
>
> "What do you mean?" I asked.
>
> "If He could trust us not to steal the glory for ourselves."
>
> Then the midnight air rang with his cry, at the top of his voice, "Not unto us, O Lord, not unto us, but unto Thy name give the glory."[10]

Can God trust us with his glory? The more God-centered we become, the more clearly we know ourselves, and we answer that question: "I cannot be trusted. I need God's help." God delights to help those who confess this kind of weakness.

But a God-centered life can be costly. Many Christians have had to choose between the glory of God and the happiness of those they love. Brother Yun was imprisoned for four years by the Chinese Communists in the 1980s. During his imprisonment, there was no one to provide for his family. He agonized each time his wife and children visited him as he witnessed their great poverty. They suffered greatly because of his stand for Christ. He could have ended their pain by denouncing Christ, but that was not an option because he lived for the glory of God rather than the happiness of others, even those closest to him.[11]

Our only hope is that the Divine nature, energized by repentance and self-abasement, will increasingly inflame us with a longing to live for the Father's glory. The repentance that proceeds from new birth is the antidote.

Jesus' Means to God's Ends

Christ's approach to his cross displays God's purpose for life, and it also shows us how to achieve that purpose. At the cross we see God pursuing heavenly ends with heavenly means.

A few days before Jesus' death, some Greeks asked for an audience with Jesus. You and I would have seen their request as an opportunity to expand our ministry to a foreign country. But Jesus didn't see it that way. He gave this unusual answer:

> The hour has come for the Son of Man to be glorified. I tell you the truth, unless a kernel of wheat falls to the ground and dies, it remains only a single seed. But if it dies, it produces many seeds. The man who loves his life will lose it, while the man who hates his life in this world will keep it for eternal life. Whoever serves me must follow me; and where I am, my servant also will be. My Father will honor the one who serves me.
>
> John 12:23–26

This passage describes God's means to his ends. He achieves his ends by dying.[12] Jesus was clear about his ultimate purpose and how to achieve it. Glory is the end; death is the means. He would reach the Greeks, but it would be by losing his life on the next day rather than entertaining their adulation for a day.

Two principles stand out in this passage. First, Jesus glorified God by sacrificing his own life and body. His body was a seed. Seeds do not grow until they go into the ground and die. The entire two-thousand-year history of the church is one seed dying and becoming one hundred, one hundred dying to become ten thousand, ten thousand dying to become one million. "This is to my Father's glory, that you bear much fruit, showing yourselves to be my disciples" (John 15:8).

Second, the perceptive church imitates Christ's ends and means. There is no other way to glorify him. God gives us opportunities to die every day. It is the little daily deaths that prepare us for the big ones, like martyrdom.

For example, husbands glorify God when they switch the TV from Monday Night Football to their wife's favorite romantic comedy. Wives glorify God when they submit to their husband's spiritual leadership despite the fact that they have a better way. Disciples glorify God when they rise early to read his Word and pray. We glorify God when we tithe in times of financial need. We glorify God when we serve and obey inconsiderate, unappreciative employers. We glorify God when we forgive a brother or sister who has repeatedly rejected us. Obedience always involves death. And death always produces the life that glorifies God.

The good news is that death ultimately ends in joy. "For the joy set before him," it says of Jesus, he "endured the cross" (Heb. 12:2). That is because saving faith perceives God's liberality and trusts that God cannot be out-given.

The great eighteenth-century evangelist George Whitefield was used by God to convert several hundred thousand people. For thirty-five years he preached an average of three sermons per day, many of them two hours long,[13] and most of the time to immense crowds in the open air, sometimes in inclement weather, shouting at the top of his lungs. The physical strain was so great that, from his mid-thirties on, he often coughed up blood for thirty minutes after preaching.[14] But this did not deter him. His great death to self produced a harvest of life for the glory of God.

"For we who are alive are always being given over to death *for Jesus' sake,* so that his life may be revealed in our mortal body. So then, death is at work in us, but life is at work in you" (2 Cor. 4:11–12, emphasis mine). God is glorified to the degree of our death to self.

Conclusion

The cross reminds us that Christianity is about God, not us. The cross reveals a radical orientation, unknown to fallen humanity. We understand it by fixing "our eyes on Jesus, the author and perfecter of our faith" (Heb. 12:2).

Although we have all sinned and fallen short of this noble objective, God imputes the perfections of Christ's motives to us when we believe. He also gives us a share of Christ's heart and motive through the miracle of New Birth. We receive the Holy Spirit, God's life, a new nature zealous for his glory, so that we can increasingly pursue God's ends with God's means. If this is not working in us, something is wrong.

Like all successful business people, Christians must become clear about their ultimate purpose and how to achieve it. They must strive to never confuse the ends and means.

6

Crucified Flesh

There is one thing we all must do if we are to be servants, and that is look to the cross. It is the crowning event of Christ's servant life. . . . Here is one secret of successful ministry.

When we keep our eyes upon the cross, we want to serve.

Kent and Barbara Hughes

Every Christian wrestles with three enemies—the flesh, the devil, and the world. In the next three chapters, we'll explore each enemy in detail.

Whether in small matters or large, repeated failure can dishearten even the most stalwart Christian. One Sunday morning I gave a sermon on the importance of selflessness. Later that night I was lying in a warm, comfortable bed, enjoying a good book.

"Would you go into the front room and get me an aspirin?" my wife politely asked.

I thought of my sermon. Then I thought of my cozy blankets and my good book. After a short hesitation I answered, "Could you get it yourself?"

We've all experienced similar self-disappointment. Whether we struggle with the more obvious sins of drug or sexual addiction, or the subtle but equally evil sins of gossip or gluttony, the flesh is a persistent enemy. Where are the resources to conquer this insidious foe?

Our hope lies at the foot of the cross. Everyone who really understands and applies the cross message increasingly conquers the flesh with its lusts and self-centered desires.

"Christianity is not difficult," an old friend observed. "It is impossible." We become especially convinced of this statement when we stare down the roaring throat of the gospel's demands. "If anyone comes to me and does not hate his father and mother, his wife and children, his brothers and sisters—yes, even his own life—he *cannot be my disciple.* . . . In the same way, any of you who does not give up everything he has *cannot be my disciple*" (Luke 14:26, 33, emphasis mine).

Jesus expects his disciples to commit and sacrifice all for his kingdom. But there is good news. Jesus knows we cannot meet these expectations in the power of human strength alone. Only the cross of Christ can empower us to overcome our selfish, fallen natures.

The Power of Desire

Campus Crusade once asked me to speak at a local university. "What would you like me to talk about?" I asked.

"We aren't practicing the spiritual disciplines as we should be. We aren't praying and reading our Bibles," the advisor admitted with discouragement.

They wanted a "how to" lecture on self-discipline, but I exhorted them to build up their desires for God. I encouraged them to see Jesus Christ as a treasure buried in the field, for which all is worth selling (Matt. 13:44–46).

Few of us lack self-discipline. Rather, we lack consistent, determined desire. All of us find it easy to discipline ourselves to do those things that we like to do. I don't have to push myself to go to football games. My wife doesn't screw up all of her willpower to watch romantic comedies.

Understanding this principle is the key to sanctification. If you loved to read your Bible and craved time alone with God in prayer, you would not need "discipline" to follow Christ. In fact, you would need discipline to *not* do these things when other responsibilities beckoned. God made us with passionate desires, and he means them to rule us.

God has engineered us to pursue our happiness, and this desire does not change at conversion. In fact, God means for conversion to intensify it. Ultimately, we do what makes us happy.[1] Long ago Augustine observed:

> For the sake of driving away unhappiness and obtaining happiness, all men do whatever they do, good or bad; they invariably, you see, want to be happy; but not all attain to what all desire. All wish to be happy; none will be so but those who wish to be good.[2]

Christian conversion does not take a detour around our desire for happiness: It goes through it. Conversion changes our conviction about *what* will make us happy. It gives us a growing confidence that in God alone is ultimate happiness. "Man has a natural craving and thirst after happiness," noted Jonathan Edwards, "and will thirst and crave, till his capacity is filled. And his capacity is of vast extent; and nothing but an infinite good can fill and satisfy his desires."[3]

Before conversion we look to a new car, a promotion, or a Caribbean cruise for fulfillment. But New Birth is radical. It increasingly convinces us that only knowing Christ will satisfy our deepest long-ings. Twenty-six hundred years ago, Ezekiel prophesied this effect. "I will give you a new heart and put a new spirit in you; I will remove from you your heart of stone and give you a heart of flesh. And I will put my Spirit in you and *move you* to follow my decrees and be careful to keep my laws" (Ezek. 36:26–27, emphasis mine).

In other words, New Birth initiates us into a supernatural life crowned with heavenly longings. The New Creation (another term for New Birth) increasingly wants to "count itself dead" and deny self for Christ and his kingdom.

Paul wrote the Galatians, "But I say, walk by the Spirit, and you will not carry out the desire of the flesh. For the flesh sets its desire against the Spirit, and the Spirit against the flesh; for these are in opposition to one another, so that you may not do the things that you please" (Gal. 5:16–17 NASB).

Paul's point is that before conversion the desires of the flesh had no competition. Afterwards, the new desires from God's Spirit stood up to and opposed the lusts of the flesh. The heart became a battleground between warring desires—each looking to a different deity for ultimate satisfaction.

As I've said before, we do not lack self-discipline; we lack desire. The hatred of sin, the love of God, and a passion to be holy—all strong desires—come from the Holy Spirit. John calls it abiding in Christ. We will use that term. These desires begin at New Birth and grow as we "live" or "walk" in the Spirit. And the most important thing we can do to live in the Spirit is meditate on his cross. Before we look at the cross, let's discuss what it means to live in the Spirit or abide in Christ.

Abiding in Christ

"When the going gets tough, the tough get going." Every day in junior high, my teammates and I ran under this sign on our way from the locker room to the football field. But this slogan does not apply to Christianity. The Christian who lives by his willpower alone will not grow in holiness. Rather, when the going gets tough, those who abide in Christ are the ones who get going. When we were converted, God united us with Christ. Our continuing responsibility is to appropriate the power of the Holy Spirit by abiding in that union. Those who do so grow in holiness. Paul calls abiding in Christ walking in the Spirit.

Four important Scriptures describe how we abide in Christ and appropriate this power.

"If a man remains in me and I in him, he will bear much fruit; apart from me you can do nothing" (John 15:5).

"The requirement of the Law [is] fulfilled in us, who do not walk according to the flesh but according to the Spirit" (Rom. 8:4 NASB).

"For if you are living according to the flesh, you must die; but if by the Spirit you are putting to death the deeds of the body, you will live" (Rom. 8:13 NASB).

"But I say, walk by the Spirit, and you will not carry out the desire of the flesh" (Gal. 5:16 NASB).

Both John and Paul overcame carnality by abiding in Christ's life, and the power of the Spirit changed them. This process requires both our active repentance and God's supernatural power.

Once I wanted to turn a small lot infested with weeds into healthy grass. First, I sowed grass seed among the weeds. Then I began to apply weed and feed each spring and fall. This product slowly poisoned the weeds and nourished the grass. Now my small plot is gradually coming around—the weeds are dying and the grass is growing.

In the same way, at conversion God plants in us a new set of desires. Those who abide in Christ daily apply spiritual weed and feed to their hearts. They mind the things of the Holy Spirit (Rom. 8:5) and put to death the deeds of the flesh (Rom. 8:13). Eventually their hearts becomes a garden dominated by healthy desires for the things that please God.

Abiding in Christ (walking in the Holy Spirit), then, is the process of feeding God's desires while poisoning our carnal yearnings. We as Christians live in God's Spirit when we set our minds "on what the Spirit desires" (Rom. 8:5). Each time we set our minds on what God wants and repent of lesser motives, we feed our spirits and poison the flesh. Our longing for God grows, swallowing up lesser desires. As this happens we move from naked self-discipline to a life of holy panting after God.[4]

Another way to say all this is that we overcome the flesh by gazing at Christ. God inflames holy desires as we see the glory of God in the face of Christ. No one can really see God this way and not long to know and serve him. It is the natural process of sanctification. "And we, who with unveiled faces all reflect the Lord's glory, are being transformed into his likeness with ever-increasing glory, which comes from the Lord, who is the Spirit" (2 Cor. 3:18).

In other words, what we behold forms us. We become like what we worship.[5] Those who worship self become self-centered. Those who worship the culture adopt the values of that culture. The best place to be transformed by the glory of God in the face of Christ is the cross. Cross-centered Christians abide in Christ.

A Passion to Flee Sin

Seeing the cross strengthens our desires two ways. First, it motivates us negatively—to hate sin, mourn for sin, and fear God. Second, it motivates us positively—to love, to forgive, to be gracious, to be lowly, and to be meek. Let's examine the negative motivations first.

90

First, the cross teaches us to fear God. The fear of God is a strong, virtue-producing desire that has great cleansing power. We should purify ourselves "from all defilement of flesh and spirit, perfecting holiness in the fear of God" (2 Cor. 7:1 NASB).

Many think that the fear of God is an Old Testament concept and don't know what to do with it today. But the cross provides the most important rationale and motivation for the fear of God. In fact, when Paul exhorts us to "work out [our] salvation with fear and trembling" (Phil. 2:12), his eye is on the cross. From it he extracts the fear of God, and this fear is a strong inducement to holiness.

A friend told me how the fear of God saved him from adultery. A woman tried to seduce him on a business trip. In the crucible of temptation he forgot both his love for God and his wife. What saved him? He remembered how David suffered after his sin with Bathsheba, and he knew he would pay the same or a greater price as he remembered how God displayed his hatred of sin at the cross. By the fear of God he "perfected holiness." Where do we get the fear of God? The cross teaches both God's hatred of sin and the costliness of sin—two truths that continually inspire us to fear him. God hates sin. No one can see God's hatred of sin, revealed at the cross, and not feel his lusts scorched as with a spiritual blowtorch. "Our sin must be extremely horrible," notes John Stott. "Nothing reveals the gravity of sin like the cross."[6]

When I was twelve my brothers and I were sleeping out in the backyard. I called my brother a word that I had heard on the playground but that I did not understand. My brother ran into the house and yelled, "Daddy, Daddy, Billy called me a _____."

I'll never forget my dad's reaction. He stormed out of the house, grabbed me by the shoulders, shook me, and in a solemn, angry voice warned me never to utter that word again. When I saw my father's intense hatred of this word, I internalized his feelings for it. That was forty-one years ago, and I have never used that word flippantly since.

The cross also motivates us negatively in a second way. It shows us the cost of sin. I did not really fear sin until I saw what it cost God to redeem me from it. It required a sacrifice of infinite value to set right the scales of divine justice. In other words, what I consider to be small sins are extremely loathsome to God.

So it is with the cross. When we see sin at the cross we see it as our Father sees it, and everything changes. Before, we were careless about sin. Now, we fear it. This fear dramatically turns us from evil.

Not only does the cross teach us to fear God, but it also makes us mourn for sin. There is little mourning for sin in today's church because the cross is not at the center of our teaching and meditations. But, Jesus promised, "Blessed are those who mourn, for they will be comforted" (Matt. 5:4). Jesus is not referring to mourning for the personal cost of sin (although the personal cost is great). This blessing belongs to those who mourn for what sin does to God, his kingdom, and his glory.

Zechariah foresaw that the cross would be the ground of our mourning:

> They will look on me, the one they have pierced, and they will mourn for him as one mourns for an only child, and grieve bitterly for him as one grieves for a firstborn son. On that day the weeping in Jerusalem will be great, like the weeping of Hadad Rimmon in the plain of Megiddo. The land will mourn, each clan by itself.
>
> Zechariah 12:10–12

No one can mourn this way for sin and remain unaffected. In fact, one important way we can measure the depth of the Holy Spirit's work is by the extent of our mourning for sin and fear of God.

We are dependent on God to show us the cross in such a way that mourning results. He revealed himself in 1949 on the Isle of Lewis, off western Scotland, through the ministry of Duncan Campbell.

> The awful presence of God brought a wave of conviction of sin that caused even mature Christians to feel their sinfulness, bringing groans of distress and prayers of repentance from the unconverted. Strong men were bowed under the weight of sin and cries for mercy were mingled with shouts of joy from others who had passed into life.[7]

Although both the fear of God and mourning for sin are negative drives and emotions, they are holy desires, placed in our hearts to overcome the lusts of the flesh. We acquire them by meditating on the cross and all that it says about God's perspective on sin.

A Passion to Be Holy

The cross also inflames positive desires. Before them, the lusts of the flesh are increasingly weak. We could describe many desires, but we will content ourselves with three: a passion to be lowly, a desire to be gracious, and a hunger for meekness.

First, the cross inflames us with a passion to be lowly. Paul's great discourse in the second chapter of Philippians details Christ's voluntary descent. Jesus surrendered equality with God and took a human body and personality. Even though equal in value to the Father, he submitted himself to his Father's will and agreed to die. (Remember, death is the penalty for sin, and he was sinless.) He submitted to crucifixion on the edge of a garbage dump[8] outside the walls of Jerusalem.

Because Christ was infinite in dignity, glory, and power, he had to descend an infinite distance to save us. You can't see this truth with the eye of your heart and not increasingly want to imitate him. Cross-focused Christians increasingly seek ways to descend in order to serve God and man.

Second, the cross gives us a desire to be gracious. The cross is the rationale for all human grace and mercy. At the cross Jesus considered us more important than himself (Phil. 2:3). And cross-focused Christians increasingly count others as more important than themselves. All who really see what they deserve and what God has done to save them want to show the same mercy to others.

I knew a group of Christians who believed in the cross but didn't emphasize it. They didn't stress what the cross teaches about our sin and unworthiness to be loved by God. It was not surprising that this group was especially critical of other Christians. The grace that crucifies a critical spirit proceeds from an emphasis upon the cross. They lacked that emphasis.

Third, the cross makes us hungry for meekness.[9] Jesus said, "Blessed are the meek, for they will inherit the earth" (Matt. 5:5). Meekness is the capacity to rejoice in adverse circumstances because we know that God controls every event, even unpleasant ones, for our ultimate good. When the engine in your car blows up in a snowstorm, meekness rejoices. When an unexpected bill arrives from the IRS, meekness does not throw a fit. Why? Because it beholds Christ's meekness at the cross and longs to imitate him.

"He was oppressed and afflicted, yet he did not open his mouth; he was led like a lamb to the slaughter, and as a sheep before her shearers is silent, so he did not open his mouth" (Isa. 53:7). There it is—utter meekness. The only man with a right to complain and fight back didn't.

Many people have appropriated God's power this way. They abide in Christ by fixing their thoughts on the cross of Christ

—living in his Spirit. For them self-denial and daily death have been grounds for great rejoicing.

John Bunyan, the author of *Pilgrim's Progress*, felt called and bound by God to preach. When he refused to cease and desist, the English government jailed him for twelve years, from age thirty to forty-two.

Seventeenth-century English jail life was not pleasant. Bunyan lived in a lice-infested environment with poor sanitation and little privacy. Fellow prisoners died of diseases easily cured today.

Despite these personal hardships, the fate of his wife and children was his greatest concern. There was no welfare in 1660 to provide for them in his absence, so he cast his family upon the mercy of his small congregation and the charity of a few friends. He stood by while his children grew up without their father. But his greatest anxiety was for his oldest daughter, who was born blind. He was closest to her. Later he wrote:

I was made to see that if ever I would suffer rightly I must first pass a sentence of death upon everything which can properly be called a thing of this life, even to reckon myself, my Wife, my Children, my Health, my Enjoyments, and all, as dead to me and myself as dead to them. And second to live upon God that is invisible.[10]

While he was imprisoned his blind daughter died. The grief almost undid him.

Bunyan knew the cost of discipleship. He knew what it meant to deny himself, take up his cross, and follow Christ. Where did he find power to live this way? He found it at the cross.

Out of this voluntary death came resurrection life. *Pilgrim's Progress*, written while in jail, has become one of history's best-selling books. Only the Bible has been translated into more languages.

Important Implications

All of this has important implications. First, if knowing, understanding, and seeing God's work at the cross is a key to sanctification, then it is imperative that we preach the cross.

A friend once told me, "I don't think Jack would make a good pastor."

"Why do you say that?" I asked.

"Because preaching is so important to him," he responded. "Pastors are counselors and friends."

"I agree that Jack's counseling skills might be weak," I answered. "But the most important thing any pastor can do is preach Christ and his cross. That is the great need of the church, and Jack is good at that. Obviously counseling and listening are also involved. But these are secondary to the one great task—preaching Christ crucified."

Many Christians have forgotten the importance of preaching. The best way to help God's people grow in holiness is to regularly preach Christ crucified. This message affects hearts, changes desires, and reorients lives. If beholding the glory of God in the cross is a crucial key to overcoming the flesh, then preaching "Jesus Christ and him crucified" (1 Cor. 2:2) is imperative.

Second, cross-centered counseling helps people in their problems. Show the guilty God's unlimited forgiveness. Show the discouraged Christ's unearnable, unchanging, never-quenchable love. Show the unrepentant God's hatred of sin. Sanctification begins and ends at the cross. Counselors who want to see lives change feed their counselees Christ crucified.

Third, find and read books about the cross. You may have some difficulty with this, since few good books on the subject have been written in the last one hundred years. John Piper has identified the reason: "I have to admit that most of my soul's food comes from very old books. I find the atmosphere of my own century far too dense with man and distant from the sweet sovereignty of God."[11]

The cross offends the modern drive to base self-esteem, self-love, and human dignity on human performance and innate goodness.

Conclusion

Christianity is not difficult, it is impossible. Naked will is insufficient. We must appropriate the power of the Holy Spirit to overcome the flesh; the power of the cross is our only hope for corporate and personal change. That is where I go when worldly desire, selfishness, and lust assail me. And that is the socket I plug myself into to acquire the power of the Holy Spirit.

God changes us from the inside out—by changing our desires. This job is too big for us; only the power of the Holy Spirit can get the job done. And God gives that power to those who live and walk in His Spirit—who unite their lives increasingly with the life of Christ. The Christian who focuses on the cross and walks in repentance lives in God's Spirit. He has most effectively united himself to Christ. He has discovered the secret to real change.

7

God's Spiritual Boot Camp

What looks like (and indeed was) the defeat of Goodness
by evil is also, and more certainly, the defeat of evil by
Goodness. Overcome there, he was himself overcoming.
Crushed by the ruthless power of Rome, he was himself
crushing the serpent's head (Gen. 3:15). The victim was
the victor, and the cross is still the throne from which he
rules the world.

John Stott

There is power in the cross to overcome and conquer the flesh.
But the flesh is just the beginning of our problems. "Our
struggle is not against flesh and blood," wrote Paul, "but against
the rulers, against the authorities, against the powers of this dark
world and against the spiritual forces of evil in the heavenly realms"
(Eph. 6:12). Yes, arrayed against us are unseen spiritual entities
with the intimidating titles of "rulers," "authorities," and "powers." We cannot fight them in our own strength.

Like many, I believed in the reality of this conflict. In theory, I knew evil spirits were out there. Then one unforgettable Sunday morning everything changed.

My wife and I went through our normal routine of feeding and dressing our five children and hurrying to get to church on time. We heard an excellent sermon from John 15 about the importance of abiding in the Vine. Afterward, the guest speaker invited those who wanted prayer for special needs to come forward.

I was an elder and headed one of the prayer teams. A teenaged girl came forward and asked us to pray for her eating habits. (We learned later that she had been struggling with bulimia and anorexia.) We laid hands on her, and to cover all of our bases, one of the men commanded any unclean spirits to quit oppressing her. This was our normal procedure. But to our surprise she immediately went into a trancelike condition and swooned to the floor. A James Earl Jones–like voice spoke out of her mouth: "I am starvation. This woman is my house, and I am not leaving."

I was stunned. I had read about these kinds of encounters, but I had never experienced one myself. Not knowing what to do but feeling responsible to do something, I blurted out nervously, "In Jesus' name, I command you to leave her, now."

"I am not leaving. I live here. This is my house," the spirit growled back in a deep, guttural voice.

Her semiconscious body began to writhe on the floor like a snake. The other men joined in with me, commanding the spirit, "In Jesus' name, leave her now." Each time they said "Jesus' name" her whole body shook as if someone had kicked her. Occasionally the spirit responded, "Don't say the name. I hate that name."

The stubborn spirit resisted us for about fifteen minutes. Finally, he left. When she came back to her senses I asked her if she had been aware of what was going on. "Vaguely," she said.

The amazing part of this story is that throughout the sanctuary similar encounters were taking place. Remember, none of us had experienced demonic encounters before. *What has happened to our peaceful little congregation?* I thought. *Where did all of this come from?* Meanwhile, our shocked congregation was frozen to their seats—a mixture of fear and fascination at work in most. Although this happened fifteen years ago, my children all vividly remember the details.

That day God in his mercy, and for his sovereign purposes, peeled back the fragile curtain separating the material realm from the spiritual, and I got a firsthand look at the intense behind-the-scenes war that rages all around us. In this case, the oppressed were believers, and none of it was staged. It sensitized me to the spiritual conflict that daily rages in this world.

Spiritual Disciplines Needed

Although most Christians engage in spiritual warfare daily, they do not need the kind of power encounter just described to walk in liberty. They need to resist the devil by applying the spiritual disciplines. This is what James had in mind when he wrote, "Resist the devil, and he will flee from you" (James 4:7).

Effective resistance demands a holy sobriety about demonic temptation that the church often lacks. Speaking from personal experience, Peter wrote,[1] "Be of sober spirit, be on the alert. Your adversary, the devil, prowls around like a roaring lion, seeking someone to devour" (1 Peter 5:8 NASB).

The best way to become "sober of spirit" and "alert" to spiritual conflict is by looking at the epic battle that took place at the cross. There Christ conquered and subdued our ancient enemy, and he used heavenly weapons to do so. We must consider Jesus' means carefully, because we conquer with the same weapons and strategies today. We learn how to fight the good fight of the faith (1 Tim. 6:12) by looking to the cross.

When we think of conflict, the first thing that comes to mind is aggression. But that was the last thing on Jesus' mind. Christ used three spiritual weapons to conquer his evil adversary.

- Faith in the Truth. In Ephesians 6:10–18 Paul refers to it defensively as the shield of faith and offensively as the sword of truth.
- Hope in his Father's willingness to reward. Paul calls hope the helmet of salvation (Eph. 6:17).
- Love displayed by obedience. "They did not love their lives so much as to shrink from death" (Rev. 12:11).

In other words, the three cardinal virtues—faith, hope, and love—were his basic weapons.[2] I want to focus on these, rather than power encounters with the devil, because in my experience, all our efforts to resist the devil are of no avail unless we grow in faith, hope, and love.

In the ensuing paragraphs, remember three things. First, we fight on two battlefields. The first is inward—in our own soul—and the second is the outside world. God wants us to use these three weapons inwardly and outwardly—plundering both realms for Christ and his kingdom.

Second, the cross does not tell us everything we need to know about spiritual warfare. The rest of the Bible is needed for that. But the cross is the best place to start.

Third, the devil has many weapons. He speaks lies, half-truths, and distortions. He orchestrates persecution through secular government, fallen men, and religious institutions. He seduces the saints. Do not be naïve about this truth. Remember, the Jewish religion and the Roman government cooperated, under Satan's tutelage, to crucify Jesus. They were the devil's instruments, but his hateful and murderous heart was behind it all.

Satan can also afflict us with diseases such as deafness, inability to speak (Mark 9:25), seizures and epilepsy (Matt. 17:14–21), fevers (Luke 4:38–39), and mental insanity (Matt. 8:28–34). He can orchestrate financial disaster, the death of loved ones, windstorms, and war (Job 1:13–19). Most importantly, he can harden human hearts so that they cannot respond to the gospel (2 Cor. 4:3–4). Demonic oppression can appear in many forms, and Satan summed these up in his oppression of Christ at the cross.

Faith in the Truth

First, Jesus conquered by believing God. He used the shield of faith and the sword of truth (Eph. 6:16–17). He clung to God's absolute goodness and sovereignty. He used faith in God's Word to repel the assaults of the enemy and to attack the enemy. "Take the helmet of salvation and the *sword of the Spirit, which is the word of God*" (Eph. 6:17, emphasis mine). God's truth is a mighty weapon. It is God's battle tank, and Satan hates it. Those who believe in its potency use it, especially when they don't feel like it is true.

The weapon of faith is crucial because Satan's most potent weapons against us are lies and half-truths. "He is a liar and the father of lies," noted Jesus (John 8:44). Satan suggests lies to us, and unless we are discerning, we think they are just our thoughts: *God doesn't love you. Does God really exist? He doesn't answer prayer. You must make it on your own. Your sins are unforgivable. Life is hopeless.*

Because Jesus bore our sin, God forsook him. Satan must have hurled a salvo of despair, discouragement, and half-truths at our Savior. In short, the devil tempted Jesus to doubt his Father's goodness and sovereignty. Because he was fully man, it was a real temptation. "My God, my God, why have you forsaken me?" Jesus cried in despair (Ps. 22:1; Matt. 27:46).

The Gospels quote Psalm 22:1, 8, 18 as direct prophecies of Christ's experience on the cross. Therefore, many Christian

103

thinkers see the entire psalm as prophetic of Christ's feelings and thoughts during his crucifixion and exaltation.[3] Verses 3–5 are a good example. Like us at times, he felt abandoned. His prayer seemed to bounce off the heavens. He looked into a terrible pit of despair. *What if the Father abandons me to hell?* he might have wondered. Then he resolved to believe the truth. "Yet you are enthroned as the Holy One; you are the praise of Israel. In you our fathers put their trust; they trusted and you delivered them. They cried to you and were saved; in you they trusted and were not disappointed" (Ps. 22:3–5).

But at the cross Jesus modeled what it is like to place our faith in God's truth even when it doesn't feel true. "He was oppressed and afflicted, yet he did not open his mouth" (Isa. 53:7). With great power and authority Jesus resisted the devil's lie and believed the truth. He worshipped God in the midst of profound pain and despair, and he did so in circumstances infinitely more difficult than you or I will ever face.

When we feel defeated, despairing under an avalanche of twisted emotions and demonic lies, the truth is the only weapon before which the devil, and our feelings, cannot stand. At these times we can always stand on rock-solid Scriptures like these: "We know that in all things God works for the good of those who love him, who have been called according to his purpose" (Rom. 8:28). "If God is for us, who can be against us?" (Rom. 8:31). "Who [or what] shall separate us from the love of Christ?" (Rom. 8:35).

Jesus battled discouragement and despair. He clung by faith to the knowledge of his Father's sovereignty and goodness. He determined to believe that God was in complete control of the cross—that he would use it all for good. He stood on the truth of Acts 2:23–24: "This Man, delivered over by the *predetermined plan* and foreknowledge of God, you nailed to a cross by the hands of godless men and put Him to death" (NASB, emphasis mine).

Jesus believed that the Father, not the devil, had predetermined his suffering, and that God was infinitely good. Without faith in these two truths—the sovereignty and love of God—we cannot stand before our adversary either. It is upon these two legs that we stand firm on the day of evil (Eph. 6:14).

Remember, Satan is like a dog on a leash, and God controls the length of the leash. For instance, the devil required God's permission to tempt Job. "The LORD said to Satan, 'Very well, then, everything he [Job] has is in your hands, but on the man himself do not lay a finger'" (Job 1:12). The devil needed God's permission to tempt Peter. "Simon, Simon, Satan has *asked* to sift you as wheat. But I have prayed for you, Simon, that your faith may not fail" (Luke 22:31–32, emphasis mine). In the same way, he must ask God to tempt or oppress you and me.

What the Bible doesn't tell us is that when Jesus uttered these words to Peter, he knew that Satan had also asked for permission to crucify him. And he knew that, in great anguish, the Father had given it. Why? Because "God so loved the world." This is why we have such great confidence in God's compassion. Whenever we suffer the effects of spiritual warfare, we have the confidence that comes from the assurance that Jesus went before us.

The Bible tells us that throughout his life, and especially at his cross, Jesus was tempted in all things as we are (Heb. 4:15) and sympathizes with our weaknesses. This is why we can have such great confidence in God's compassion. Whenever we suffer the effects of spiritual warfare, we have the confidence that comes from the assurance that Jesus went before us.

The question is not whether we will have trials. The question is when and how difficult the trials will be. Those with rock-solid, unshakable faith in God's goodness and God's sovereignty over their trials will be unshaken by the devil's seduction.

Sometimes God's people suffer greatly. The devil once asked for the great Chinese evangelist, Watchman Nee (1903–72), and for reasons known only to God, Satan got his request. Nee spent the last twenty years of his life in a communist prison, but he persevered to the end, dying victorious. Even though he was forbidden to mention God, his last letter out of prison read, "In my sickness I still remain joyful at heart." After his death the guards found under his pillow a piece of paper with the following written in a shaky hand: "Christ is the Son of God who died for the redemption of sinners and resurrected after three days. This is the greatest truth in the universe. I die because of my belief in Christ. Watchman Nee."[4]

So take heart. God has not guaranteed us a walk down easy street, but he does guarantee a purposeful, fruitful life for his glory. Like Christ at his cross; we overcome Satan by believing the truth.

Do you have a rebellious child? God is sovereign and good. Are you suffering repeated sickness? God is sovereign and good. Is your business in bankruptcy? Are you depressed and despairing? God is sovereign and good. Satan will do everything in his power to get you to disbelieve these two basic truths. This is the "testing of our faith" mentioned in James 1:3. Trials do not test our faith in God's existence. Trials test our faith in his goodness and his sovereignty.

Although we also know that our sufferings and trials are under God's sovereign control, Satan will do everything in his power to dissuade us of this nourishing truth. Resist him with faith in God's Word.

Hope in God's Goodness

Jesus' second weapon was hope in his Father's goodness. That is why Paul tells us to wear "the helmet of salvation" (Eph. 6:17). The hope of future reward should surround our mind like a helmet (1 Thess. 5:8).

106

I recently was commiserating with a Christian in the prime of life who had been diagnosed with Parkinson's disease. He is athletic, tall, handsome, and very active. Secretly, I felt sorry for him. Expecting him to complain, I asked how he was feeling. To my surprise, with a knowing smile he answered, "God has blessed me despite my disease."

He could say this because he had anchored his hope in God's promise to someday replace his dying body with an immortal, incorruptible one. This saint knew that his affliction was no accident, and that ultimately, good things awaited him. His hope was in God, and God was sovereign over his problems.

Faith and hope are closely related. As we have seen, saving faith believes ardently that God is both good and sovereign, and hope builds its house on faith's foundation. The orientation of faith is either past or present, but hope differs in that its orientation is the future. It telescopes the horizon for reward. Notice the close connection between faith and hope in Hebrews. "Faith is the assurance of things hoped for" (Heb. 11:1 ESV). "And without faith it is impossible to please God, because anyone who comes to him must believe that he exists and that he *rewards* those who earnestly seek him" (Heb. 11:6, emphasis mine).

With the weapon of hope, Jesus fought the devil at the cross. "For the *joy set before him* [Jesus] endured the cross" (Heb. 12:2, emphasis mine). Hope in his Father's lavish rewards filled Jesus with an unquenchable joy that empowered him to endure the devil's torments and slanders. And his hope was well placed—God did not let him down (Phil. 2:9ff.).

Hope always inspires endurance. As it did for Jesus, it empowers us to patiently endure trials with our eyes on God's reward. Scripture describes how endurance is inspired by hope (1 Thess. 1:3), how hope waits patiently (Rom. 8:24–25), and how the hope that our confidence will be richly rewarded (Heb. 10:35–36) empowers us to persevere.

The more real the reward, the greater is our capacity to hope. People will endure great trials when the reward is real and tangible. Ultimately, for the Christian, the reward is God himself. He is both the gift and the giver. Therefore, hope is a byproduct of our capacity to see the glory of God in the face of Christ.[5] The more God opens the eyes of our hearts to know him, the greater our capacity for hope and the greater our perseverance.

Like Psalm 22, Psalm 69 probably takes us behind the scenes of Christ's struggle with the Evil One. For several months severe clinical depression afflicted Craig. His future was like a dreary tunnel of dense, gray clouds without light or hope. In desperation, he turned to prayer. On one occasion his Bible randomly opened to Psalm 69.

He read, "Save me, O God! For the waters have come up to my neck. I sink in deep mire, where there is no foothold; I have come into deep waters, and the flood sweeps over me. I am weary with my crying out; my throat is parched. My eyes grow dim with waiting for my God" (Ps. 69:1–3 ESV).

That's exactly how I feel, Craig thought. He continued to read, for the first time aware that God understood his battle. Then he came to the last few verses:

> I will praise God's name in song
>   and glorify him with thanksgiving.
> This will please the LORD more than an ox,
>   more than a bull with its horns and hoofs.
> The poor will see and be glad—
>   you who seek God, may your hearts live!
> The LORD hears the needy
>   and does not despise his captive people.
>
> Psalm 69:30–33

My friend was encouraged when he saw how the psalmist cut down the tentacles of despair with hope in God. Craig determined to hope himself, and by that power he persevered until, several months later, the devil was vanquished.

For you and me, hope is also a crucial weapon. Never underestimate the power of hope to disarm Satan. In a deep depression, the psalmist wrote, "Why are you downcast, O my soul? Why so disturbed within me? Put your hope in God, for I will yet praise him, my Savior and my God" (Ps. 42:5–6).

In 1498 Girolamo Savonarola was tortured for thirty days by church authorities for his criticism of the pope's immorality. Repeatedly they tied his hands behind his back, tied a rope around his wrists, lifted him to the ceiling, then dropped him, stopping with a terrible jerk just before he hit the floor, tearing his shoulders from their sockets. As the pain and fear increased, the demons must have borne down. *God has abandoned you to your own resources. This is happening because of your sin. You have displeased God. He does not love you. Your future is hopeless.*

Savonarola looked into the pit of despair, but in the end, God's grace sustained his hope. He wrote a meditation on the psalms expressing his temptation to despair.

> Where shall I turn, to whom shall I flee, I who have no one left in all the world to give me aid or solace? . . . On earth I find no refuge for I have become an object of scandal and offense to men. What then shall I do? Shall I give myself over to despair?[6]

Had he despaired he would have denied Christ and compromised his life's work. But Savonarola conquered the tormenting spirits by hoping in his Master's lavish rewards. He answered his own question:

> God abundantly pardons, my redeemer is full of mercy. God alone is my refuge, He will not abandon the work of his hands and the human being made in his image.[7]

Empowered by growing hope, he persevered in suffering. Seeing that they were getting nowhere, his tormentors eventually gave up. They strangled him, hung his body in the great square in downtown Florence, and consumed it in a bonfire. Savonarola went to the heavenly reward for which he so ardently hoped. Jesus conquered the devil with hope. So do all who embrace that hope today.

Love Expressed by Obedience

The third weapon Jesus used to conquer the devil was the obedience that proceeds from love, and by this same means the church will ultimately conquer. "For they loved not their lives even unto death" (Rev. 12:11 ESV).

I have saved the most important weapon for last. To destroy the devil Jesus did not confront him. He did not aggressively attack him. Instead, he was passive toward his adversary and expressed his love for God by obedience. The devil conquered Adam by inciting disobedience, so the Second Adam conquered the devil with absolute obedience.

In short, Jesus conquered the devil by dying; the cross was Jesus' ultimate weapon. In other words, Jesus conquered the devil by letting the devil destroy him.

I just heard the story of a group of Christians in India that meet together regularly to pray for strength to die for Jesus. They face the prospect of death and physical harm every day. This weapon is real to them. It is not to those of us who live in freedom.

Love expressing itself through obedience is God's secret wisdom. It is foolishness to the worldly mind, but it is foundational to all gospel wisdom.

We preach Christ crucified, a stumbling block to Jews and folly to Gentiles, but to those who are called, both Jews and Greeks, Christ the power of God and the wisdom of God. For the foolishness of God is wiser than men, and the weakness of God is stronger than men.

I Corinthians 1:23–25 ESV

Paul had this weapon in mind when he wrote, "He was crucified in weakness, yet he lives by God's power" (2 Cor. 13:4). At the cross, God let a finite creature conquer him, and the byproduct was our salvation.

When we talk about spiritual warfare, often the weapon of love expressing itself as obedience is the last weapon discussed. We exhort one another to rebuke the devil, cast out evil spirits, intercede, or raise the shield of faith. These are all important, but the weapon of self-denial, the most important, is usually forgotten. What I am saying is that, just like Jesus, we conquer the devil and plunder his kingdom by dying. Jonathan Edwards notes:

> The weapons that Christ made use of were his poverty, afflictions and reproaches, sufferings and death. His principle weapon was his cross: the instrument of his own reproachful death. . . . With weapons as these has Christ in a human, weak, mortal nature overthrown and baffled all the craft of Hell.[8]

It is really very simple. Adam's "no" to God's will empowered the devil. Christ's "yes" to God's will conquered the devil. In the same way, our "yes" is the church's crucial weapon in the present hour.[9] The sword of faith and the helmet of hope, without this obedience, are like an M-16 with no ammunition.

Obedience is a powerful weapon for two reasons. First, God extends his kingdom into the battlefield of this fallen world on the back of our obedience. Second, the obedience of love weakens the devil's power over our personal inward battleground, rendering his assaults fruitless. We will examine these one at a time.

111

Death Extends the Gospel

Everyone empowered to plunder the devil's kingdom pays a price for it. That is why Paul wrote, "I rejoice in my sufferings for your sake, and in my flesh I do my share on behalf of his body, which is the church, in filling up what is lacking in Christ's afflictions" (Col. 1:24 NASB).

Paul did not mean that Christ's sufferings were inadequate to atone for sin. He meant that the suffering of obedience would be needed to further plunder the devil's earthly kingdom. He meant that, like his Master, he knew God would use him to subjugate the devil by dying. "Go, for he is a chosen instrument of Mine, to bear My name before the Gentiles and kings and the sons of Israel; for I will show him how much he must suffer for My name's sake" (Acts 9:15–16 NASB). In this sense his suffering filled up what is lacking in Christ's. It has ever been this way: Ultimately, this is how God spreads his gospel and extends his kingdom.

Every advance of the gospel travels over someone's willingness to die. Whether death to too much TV, the love of money, the praise of others, or worldly success, the highway over which God's triumphs travel is paved with the self-denial of his saints. It is an immutable, unchanging principle, and the cross shouts it to us with a megaphone.

Death Gives Personal Victory

Obedience that proceeds from love is also the crucial weapon in personal deliverance from the devil's power. When Jesus said, "The prince of this world is coming. He has no hold on me" (John 14:30), he meant "I have no sin that the devil can use to control me." Unless we can make this same boast, we waste our time on spiritual warfare. By this I don't mean that we need to be perfect, just repentant. Confessed sin destroys Satan's power over us; unconfessed sin invites his manipulation.

Remember, temptation begins with our desires—you can't blame it on the devil. Each lust gratified tightens the devil's grip. Each confessed sin loosens it.

> Let no one say when he is tempted, "I am being tempted by God"; for God cannot be tempted by evil, and He Himself does not tempt anyone. But each one is tempted when he is carried away and enticed by his own lust.
>
> James 1:13–14 NASB

This is why Paul went to such great lengths to maintain a clear conscience. "Now this is our boast: Our conscience testifies that we have conducted ourselves in the world, and especially in our relations with you, in the holiness and sincerity that are from God" (2 Cor. 1:12). Without this testimony Paul knew he could not walk in personal freedom from demonic oppression.

Every "yes" to God's call by a missionary, every employee's decision to serve an unjust employer, every husband's attempt to serve a premenstrual wife, every tithe check written in a time of need, every hour spent in prayer when you would rather watch TV, every decision to preach an unpopular sermon for the glory of God, every confession of sexual failure, and every attempt to forgive an enemy removes the devil's oppressive power. It extends God's kingdom just that much further. The obedience that flows out of love for God is our crucial weapon.

In this sense, the cross was the great weapon that Jesus used to conquer his enemy. Its great irony should not escape us. At the very moment Satan thought he was conquering Christ, he was actually being conquered by Jesus' willingness to die.

Conclusion

In my experience, unless we practice faith, hope, and the obedience of love, our spiritual victories will be temporary. So these weapons are crucial. The armies of heaven that follow the King of Kings and Lord of Lords never fail to use them. This army conquers for Christ in time and space.

I saw heaven standing open and there before me was a white horse, whose rider is called Faithful and True. With justice he judges and makes war. His eyes are like blazing fire, and on his head are many crowns. He has a name written on him that no one knows but he himself. He is dressed in a robe dipped in blood, and his name is the Word of God. The armies of heaven *were following him*, riding on white horses and dressed in fine linen, white and clean. Out of his mouth comes a sharp sword with which to strike down the nations. "He will rule them with an iron scepter." He treads the winepress of the fury of the wrath of God Almighty. On his robe and on his thigh he has this name written: KING OF KINGS AND LORD OF LORDS.

Rev. 19:11–16, emphasis mine

The army of God is in every nation and generation. It is an all-volunteer army. Ultimately, it is the only army in history that matters. It fights an unseen foe with spiritual weapons, and the cross is its boot camp, the place of basic training and conditioning. Have you been taught there? Have you been taught by our great General, the King of Kings and Lord of Lords? He conquered by going low. He conquered by obeying. He conquered by serving. He conquered with the shield of faith, the sword of the spirit, and the helmet of hope. And he is eager to steel your spiritual muscles to use the same spiritual weapons to advance his kingdom in our generation.

8

I Will Boast No More

Some are saying, Oh, that the world were crucified to me, and I to the world! Oh, that my heart were as dead as a stone to the world, and alive to Jesus! Do you truly wish it? Look, then, to the cross . . . gaze upon a crucified Jesus. So will the world become a dim and dying thing.

R. M. McCheyne

The cross is a key to victory over the flesh and the devil. But the cross is also a key to victory over our third enemy, the world.

At a party hosted by a Christian friend I made the acquaintance of a middle-aged gentleman. We discovered that we attended the same church.

"How long have you attended our church?" I asked.

"Seven years."

I was shocked. I had never seen this man or heard his name, yet we had attended the same church for seven years? Theoretically, this was possible. It was a growing church with two services, and

I attended the early service while he attended the later. But still, seven years?

Secretly, I was even more disappointed because he had not heard of me, even though I was chairman of the elder board and the main adult Sunday school teacher. Before the evening was over, I made sure he knew my titles and my importance.

As I was driving home the Holy Spirit brought me under conviction. I had boasted in something other than the cross of Christ—in this case, my position—and by doing so I had actually denied the cross. I had yielded to the boastful pride of life condemned by John (1 John 2:16 NASB). Although I looked spiritual on the outside, on the inside I was snared by the world and at odds with God. The god of this world had seduced me.

We can learn to overcome worldly seduction by appropriating and living in the power of the cross. Paul knew this power: "But may it never be that I would boast, except in the cross of our Lord Jesus Christ, through which the world has been crucified to me, and I to the world" (Gal. 6:14 NASB). Obviously, something about the cross empowered Paul to conquer the world, but what was it?

World Defined

Many passages exhort us to flee from the world. For example, "Do not love the world nor the things in the world. If anyone loves the world, the love of the Father is not in him" (1 John 2:15 NASB). Or how about, "You adulteresses, do you not know that friendship with the world is hostility toward God? Therefore whoever wishes to be a friend of the world makes himself an enemy of God" (James 4:4 NASB). This strong language motivates every perceptive Christian to pursue freedom from the world and its values.

But what did John and James mean by the "world" in these verses? Is a teen worldly because he participates in a mosh pit at a Christian rock concert? Is a woman worldly because she wears designer clothes? Is a man worldly because he drives a Mercedes Benz? Is a Christian couple worldly because they take dance lessons or listen to country music?

Maybe . . . but these activities themselves are not necessarily signs of worldliness.

Worldliness is too subtle to be analyzed this simply. Worldly people are those who have internalized the values of the fallen world around them. To understand worldliness, then, we must understand the values that drive the fallen world.

The "world" that John and James passionately exhort us to avoid is something very specific. It is not the physical creation or the people in the world. Rather, it is human civilization organized and operating independently from God. Independence from God is the central feature of worldliness. In other words, worldly people pursue temporal pleasures (not bad in themselves) by their own rules, for their own goals, all the while thumbing their noses at the God for whom they feel little need. According to Jerry Bridges, the world is "often used in the Bible as a shorthand expression for the sum total of human society that is in opposition to God."[1] What sets the world in opposition to God is its proud independence. In other words, to the degree that people live independently of God they are worldly. By this definition, the world is alive and well in industry, education, politics, and regretfully, even in the church.

The Mark of Worldliness

When we think of worldliness, we usually think of someone famous and irreligious like Marilyn Monroe—someone glamorous, beautiful, rich, and popular. But the *Titanic* is really a better model of worldliness, because the spirit of the *Titanic* energizes worldly behavior.

In April of 1912 the *Titanic* left England on its maiden voyage. The ship was an engineering marvel, but it only carried lifeboats for half of the 2,200 passengers on board. A false confidence deceived builders, captain, crew, and travelers. Who needs lifeboats? The *Titanic* is unsinkable! But just off Newfoundland, in 13,000 feet of ice water, the impossible happened. The luxury liner hit an iceberg and sank. The drowning of hundreds proved that the confidence of these men was seriously misplaced.

In the same way, the primary mark of worldly people is that they are on a spiritual Titanic. Sailing through life on a collision course with the judgment seat of Christ, they feel great confidence in their own goodness. They feel no need of Christ or his cross. Proud independence, therefore, not drinking and dancing, is the real heart and soul of worldliness.

I tried to share the gospel with Beth, a friend embroiled in a New Age cult. I explained that God was holy and that she was sinful. I explained that she could only get right with God by believing that Jesus died in her place to take God's wrath and give her his righteousness. She grew increasingly upset as we talked.

"I erased the word *sin* from my vocabulary many years ago," she responded. "I was never comfortable, even as a teen, with the concept of original sin. Good and bad are fabrications of humanity. God is tolerant of everyone and everything."

Beth was walking the deck of her own spiritual Titanic. Her worldliness was no different in principle from the same proud independence of a godless CEO or the unbelieving alcoholic on Main Street. Because they cannot see God's holiness or their sin, they don't feel that they need God. Their ship sails for disaster while they continue in blind arrogance. Whether regular church attendees or ardent atheists, worldly people share this one thing in common—they feel little need for the living God upon whom all their happiness depends.

In Revelation, the Whore of Babylon represents the world. Notice her heart attitude: "In her heart she boasts, 'I sit as queen;

I am not a widow, and I will never mourn'" (Rev. 18:7). Then the unthinkable happens. She hits the great iceberg of God's judgment. "Therefore in one day her plagues will overtake her: death, mourning and famine. She will be consumed by fire, for mighty is the Lord God who judges her. . . . 'In one hour her doom has come'" (Rev. 18:8, 10).

Worldly Christians

In other words, a worldly person is one who has internalized the values of unredeemed human society. The Bible calls the independence that characterizes worldliness "boasting." It is the first symptom of conformity to the world.

Worldliness also has secondary symptoms. Like the fallen world around him, the worldly person seeks meaning and fulfillment independently—in something or someone other than God. That "something" in which he seeks meaning usually includes the lust for power, the craving for possessions, and the boasting of what he possesses or has attained. "I have an MBA from Harvard." "Did you see my new Acura Legend?"

That is why the apostle John warned us, "For all that is in the world, the lust of the flesh [probably power and sex] and the lust of the eyes [for things] and the boastful pride of life, is not from the Father, but is from the world" (1 John 2:16 NASB). A worldly person seeks ultimate meaning independently—in things rather than God, who is the fountain of all true meaning and happiness.

Therefore, independent autonomy, not the clothes we wear or the cars we drive, is the heart of worldliness. Designer clothes and luxury cars could be symptoms of this independence, but you would have to know one's heart attitude to determine this, because the heart and soul of worldliness is much deeper than these. For instance, you could be dirt poor and still be intensely worldly. Independence is the problem, and this independent spirit always boasts in something or someone other than Christ.

Galatians 6:14 Unwrapped

Paul wrote Galatians to combat a false gospel that boasted in human achievement as the basis for acceptance with God rather than the cross. This false gospel was "worldly." It insisted that the Galatians could not get right with God unless they submitted to, among other things, the Jewish rite of circumcision. In other words, they preached a gospel that boasted in human works (in this case, circumcision), rather than the work of Christ at the cross for reconciliation.

Therefore, Paul ended Galatians with this conclusive statement: "May I never boast except in the cross of our Lord Jesus Christ, through which the world has been crucified to me, and I to the world" (Gal. 6:14). The Galatians' penchant for boasting in something other than God was the "world" that was crucified to Paul. There are two expressions in this verse that we need to define.

First, when he said that the world had "been crucified to me," he meant that at the cross he saw God's feelings for his worldly independence. The world was crucified in Christ. It deserved to be pierced with nails, tortured to death naked, matted in sweat and blood. When Paul saw God's abhorrence of worldliness, he shrunk back in horror.

As Paul internalized God's abhorrence for the world, he also felt antipathy toward those at home with the world and all that it valued.[2] In fact, his constant emphasis upon fallen man's helpless dependence provoked most of his horrible persecutions.[3] "Brothers, if I am still preaching circumcision," he said, "why am I still being persecuted? In that case the offense of the cross has been abolished" (Gal. 5:11). The offense of the cross was and is its statement about our utter bankruptcy.

Second, when Paul said he was crucified "to the world," he meant that he had died to worldliness. The cross had destroyed his proud self-confidence and left him absolutely dependent upon Christ for all ultimate merit and meaning. In other words, Paul saw that his worldly independence had been crucified in Christ (Gal. 2:20). Therefore, the cross had crushed and withered all grounds to boast in his achievements (even though there were many).[4] And Paul rejoiced in his newfound poverty.

Every Christian who really understands the cross boasts in Christ alone for all meaning and dignity in this life and the life to come. To the degree that we see the world through the window of the cross, we will be dead to the world. Increasingly irrelevant are the accumulation of things and pride in accomplishments. We can lay aside the need to talk about our degrees, job titles, and possessions. A Christian who boasts in the cross is dead to the search for meaning and personal fulfillment in ministry, success, money, education, or possessions.

Two assumptions about spiritual reality form the foundations upon which Galatians 6:14 stands. Properly understood, these assumptions break the back of worldliness.

Our Bankruptcy

First, the cross trumpets our moral and spiritual bankruptcy. Whenever I speak harshly to my wife, criticize a friend, fall into unbelief, or fail in some other way, I run for solace to the glorious truth that "I have been crucified with Christ" (Gal. 2:19). The cross reminds me that these sins, which I take so lightly, actually deserve crucifixion. My own righteousness is inadequate. I will either trust Jesus to be crucified in my place, or I will take a personal punishment akin to crucifixion for eternity.

Since God is perfectly just, and punishment for sin (hell) is infinite, the offense must be infinite. Therefore, apart from

121

Christ's cross I am in serious trouble. I face a problem of infinite proportions with personal resources that are at best miniscule. Those who rely upon self in the face of this problem will be utterly ruined.

No one can see the cross and continue to cruise self-confidently through life on a spiritual Titanic. Instead, all who see their infinite need urgently buckle on their life vests and rush to faith in Christ—God's spiritual lifeboat. But because our penchant for boasting is pathological, few take God's remedy. Some examples follow.

To one who boasts of his good intentions, the cross says, "Your righteousness is like filthy rags in my sight" (Isa. 64:6).

To the decent person from a respectable family who never abused drugs, drank excessively, or slept around, the cross says, "There is no one who does good, not even one" (Rom. 3:12).

To the man with great financial success, the cross says, "Let not . . . the rich man boast of his riches" (Jer. 9:23).

To the twentysomething who secretly boasts in her good looks, the cross says, "Charm is deceptive, and beauty is fleeting; but a woman who fears the LORD is to be praised" (Prov. 31:30).

To the man who boasts in his intelligence, the cross says, "Let not the wise man boast of his wisdom" (Jer. 9:23).

To the pastor who brags about the size of his church or the effect of his preaching, the cross says, "Vanity of vanities! All is vanity" (Eccles. 1:2).

"There is no one righteous, not even one" (Rom. 3:10). Christ took what I deserve; he was crucified in my place. All who boast in their ministry, good intentions, decency, position, beauty, education, or intelligence have not clearly seen the message being shouted from the cross.

To the degree that we see ourselves at the cross, we experience our need. And needy people seek God. But no one feels their need until they see their sin in God's light. "He who is full loathes honey, but to the hungry even what is bitter tastes sweet" (Prov. 27:7). The cross is where we see our sin in all its vulgarity.

Overcoming worldly boasting is a lifelong project. The closer you get to the cross, the more you will overcome it, but you will never be completely free of it in this life.

A World under Judgment

Not only does the cross show us our bankruptcy, but it also reminds us that this fallen world is under God's judgment. That is why worldly pleasure cannot satisfy our deepest longings. The cross says, "Don't look to the material world for ultimate meaning and fulfillment."

The day before his crucifixion Jesus warned, "Now is the time for judgment on this world" (John 12:31). Our worldliness was in Christ, and the Father judged it at the cross. We rejoice that Christ bore it for us. But this truth also reminds us that God will eventually judge all worldliness. Christ took that judgment for those who believe, but those who don't will bear it themselves.

That is why Scripture tells us that this fallen world awaits a future judgment.

> But the day of the Lord will come like a thief. The heavens will disappear with a roar; *the elements will be destroyed by fire*, and the earth and everything in it will be laid bare. Since everything will be destroyed in this way, what kind of people ought you to be? You ought to live holy and godly lives.
>
> 2 Peter 3:10–11, emphasis mine

This truth hit me with force on a business trip to Hawaii a few years ago. I flew on a charter with fellow sales associates whom I had known for many years. Most wore Ralph Lauren, made six-digit incomes, and drove luxury cars. Many were on second and third marriages. Others were depressed and morose. One husband was in an adulterous relationship with his secretary. Few were genuinely happy. I had watched them rise in their careers over twenty years, but their happiness had not risen with their financial status. This world's inability to deliver the happiness it promised had never been more real to me.

A delicate bouquet of fresh-cut orchids graced the coffee table in our hotel suite. After admiring them, I randomly opened my Bible to get my mind off of these problems. My eyes fell on this passage:

> All men are like grass,
>   and all their glory is like the flowers of the field.
> The grass withers and the flowers fall
>   because the breath of the Lord blows on them.
> Surely the people are grass . . .
>   but the word of our God stands forever.
>
> Isaiah 40:6–8

I looked back at the fragile flowers. They were beautiful, but they would surely wilt by tomorrow.

The message was clear. The happiness and fulfillment that this world promises has the substance and staying power of fresh-cut orchids wilting under a tropical sun. They will wither, droop, and perish under God's judgment. Always thinking that just a little bit more will satisfy, the world's promises had already withered for my friends. God only gives the reward of ultimate satisfaction to those who make their boast in the cross of Christ.

The cross makes this truth clear. A life lived independent of God cannot possibly satisfy. Because it is under God's judgment, God won't let it satisfy. Have you ever known anyone who had just a little bit more and was happier—I mean, really happy? The tragic nature of most biographies in glamour magazines should convince those tempted with worldly desires that these things cannot deliver.

Conclusion

Looking at the cross enables us to appropriate God's power to overcome worldliness. The cross says, "Don't boast in success, wealth, education, or talent. All such boasting is vanity. It will not help on the Day of Judgment, nor will it deliver any long-term happiness."

All such boasting is a participation in independence from God, which is the heart of worldliness. It denies the vital truths proclaimed by the cross. Understanding all this, Robert McCheyne advised his congregation,

> Some are saying, Oh, that the world were crucified to me, and I to the world! Oh, that my heart were as dead as a stone to the world, and alive to Jesus! Do you truly wish it? Look, then, to the cross. Behold the amazing gift of love. Salvation is promised to a look. Sit down, like Mary, and gaze upon a crucified Jesus. So will the world become a dim and dying thing. When you gaze upon the sun, it makes everything else dark; when you taste honey, it makes everything else tasteless: so when your soul feeds on Jesus, it takes away the sweetness of all earthly things; praise, pleasure, fleshly lusts, all lose their sweetness. Keep a continued gaze. Run, looking unto Jesus. Look, till the way of salvation by Jesus fills up the whole horizon, so glorious and peace-speaking. So will the world be crucified to you, and you unto the world.[5]

I boasted about my position to a friend at a party. In a moment of weakness I acted from the principle of the world. But I want to be able to say with Paul, "May I never boast except in the cross of our Lord Jesus Christ, through which the world has been crucified to me, and I to the world" (Gal. 6:14).

9

The Foolishness of God's Wisdom

The wisdom of God hath made Christ's humiliation the means of our exaltation; his coming down from heaven hath made life the fruit of death. . . . Here favour is made to arise out of wrath . . . our everlasting blessedness, from Christ being made a curse for us. . . . By such wonderful means hath the wisdom of God procured our salvation.

Jonathan Edwards

Shortly after my conversion, I and about six other young Christians met one evening in an empty classroom at Gonzaga University. We had been reading our Bibles and had decided to pray for the spiritual gifts mentioned in 1 Corinthians 12. We joined hands and prayed fervently. Because I was naïve but very zealous, I asked for wisdom. I knew it was important, but I did not really understand why.

Even after the passing of many years I still remember that night vividly. As we prayed, I sensed the presence of God and a profound conviction that my prayer would be answered.

At that time I did not understand God's wisdom. Wisdom was gray-bearded professors in hooded gowns presiding over college commencements. Wisdom was Socrates and philosophy, Carl Sagan and deep thoughts. What I eventually received was not what I'd asked for. The cross is the wisdom of God, but I wasn't looking at the cross.

In the meantime, three Scriptures progressively led me into a new understanding of God's wisdom, an understanding that would radically change my life.

Corrupted Wisdom

The first passage was Ezekiel 28:17. Here Ezekiel describes the downfall of the king of Tyre. In the process, the Holy Spirit carries the prophet behind the scenes to Satan, the spiritual prince of Tyre, and his original fall.

> Your heart was proud because of your beauty;
>> you *corrupted your wisdom* for the sake of your splendor.
> I cast you to the ground;
>> I exposed you before kings,
>> to feast their eyes on you.
>
> ESV, emphasis mine

In what way did Satan's fall corrupt his wisdom? I wondered. Try as I might, I could see no connection between tarnished wisdom and the devil's original sin.

Earthly or Heavenly Wisdom

A few years later the following passage in the third chapter of James caught my attention.

> Who is *wise* and understanding among you? By his good conduct let him show his works in the meekness of *wisdom*. But if you have bitter jealousy and selfish ambition in your hearts, do not

boast and be false to the truth. This is not the *wisdom* that comes down from above, but is earthly, unspiritual, demonic. For where jealousy and selfish ambition exist, there will be disorder and every vile practice. But the *wisdom* from above is first pure, then peaceable, gentle, open to reason, full of mercy and good fruits, impartial and sincere. And a harvest of righteousness is sown in peace by those who make peace.

James 3:13–18 ESV, emphasis mine

James presents two wisdoms. One is from God, and its origin is heavenly. The other is from earth, and its origin is hell.

In addition, James tells us that our behavior is a window through which we can identify the nature of our wisdom. Heavenly wisdom produces humility and peace; earthly wisdom produces envy, selfish ambition, and disorder.

I was still confused. What was God's wisdom? How did it differ from earthly wisdom? Why did these different wisdoms produce such radically different fruits?

Wisdom in Christ

Last, the Holy Spirit impressed me with Colossians 2:2–3. Paul prayed that the Colossians

may know the mystery of God, namely, Christ, in whom are *hidden* all the *treasures* of *wisdom* and knowledge.

emphasis mine

This verse presented me with three vital truths that I did not understand. First, Paul tells us that wisdom is a treasure. I knew by faith that it was valuable, but I prayed for it because I wanted to know *why* wisdom was a treasure.

Second, it was *hidden.* But who hid it? Was it hidden from the church as well as the world? One thing was sure: It was hidden from me.

Third, it was hidden *in Christ.* In some mysterious way Christ's life and death revealed God's hidden treasure—wisdom—but try as I might, I could not see it in Christ. When I looked at him I saw obedience, suffering, love, and courage, but wisdom did not leap out at me.

I prayed: "Lord, I want to understand your wisdom. Help me understand why it is a treasure. Let me see your wisdom in the life and death of your Son."

Light from God

God does not operate on our timetable. Twelve years after my prayer at Gonzaga University, he began to reveal his wisdom.

For some reason that I don't remember, I purchased the seventeenth-century classic *The Existence and Attributes of God* by the Puritan scholar Stephen Charnock. Among other things, he devoted 107 pages to a detailed biblical analysis of God's wisdom. Summing up his research, he defined "heavenly wisdom" with this life-changing sentence:

> Wisdom consists in acting for a right end. . . . He is the wisest man that hath the noblest *end* and the fittest *means,* so God is infinitely wise; as he is the most excellent being, so he hath the most excellent end.[1]
>
> emphasis mine

The light went on, the dots connected, and the three passages on wisdom that had troubled me for so long synthesized into one glorious truth.

For some time I had known that God's end is his glory. To glorify himself he both created and redeemed.[2] But now, for the first time, I saw that all wisdom is the pursuit of a particular end with a specific means. God's wisdom consists in the pursuit of the perfect *end*, his glory, with the perfect *means*, an outpouring of self-sacrificing, self-humbling love. By contrast, the "earthly wisdom" mentioned by James pursues the glory of man, with corrupt means—control, manipulation, or domination.

"God's wisdom has the supremacy of God's glory as the beginning, middle, and end of it," notes John Piper.

But man's wisdom delights in seeing himself as resourceful, self-sufficient, self-determining, and not utterly dependent on God's free grace. Divine wisdom begins consciously with God, is consciously sustained by God, and has the glory of God as its conscious goal. When divine wisdom is revealed to humans, its effect is to humble us and give us the same God-orientation that God himself has.[3]

Satanic Wisdom

Armed with this understanding, I saw why, according to Ezekiel, Satan's fall had corrupted his wisdom. God created Satan with heavenly wisdom. He existed to continuously glorify God by a godly means—adoration and praise.

But when Lucifer pursued his own glory with selfish means, his wisdom twisted and corrupted itself into a perverse thing. God judged him severely and allowed this wisdom to take its natural course. Satan began to hate God's wisdom and love his own perverse version.

Adam and Eve's sin was a participation in the devil's twisted wisdom. "When the woman saw that the fruit of the tree was . . . desirable for gaining wisdom, she took some and ate it" (Gen. 3:6). In this way Satan became the "prince of this world" (John 12:31), lord and prince of each person born of human flesh. The result is that we are all born with the devil's corrupted wisdom and utterly estranged from the true wisdom that belongs to God. "Earthly" wisdom is by nature in our blood.

So it is not surprising that the wisdom of God was hidden from me. I had no capacity to see or experience God's wisdom without a radical change of nature through New Birth. Before regeneration I partook of this fallen, twisted wisdom. I pursued my own glory with corrupt means—grasping, controlling, and dominating. I advanced self at every opportunity. This wisdom so powerfully gripped me that, even after conversion, I was slow to embrace the implications of God's wisdom. I suspect I am not alone.

Wisdom in Action

Charnock's definition of heavenly wisdom also shed light on the third chapter of James. James pictures the world as a battleground for two competing wisdoms, one coming down from heaven and another coming up from the earth.

This is *why* James is so concerned with the fruit of wisdom. Since earthly wisdom pursues its own glory, its calling card is self-ish ambition. Therefore, the aroma of fallen wisdom is jealousy, envy, and schism. The unregenerate cannot have God's wisdom or a capacity to value it; their wisdom is always earthly. But God's children are a mixture of competing wisdoms—a concoction that, as we saw in chapter 6, the Holy Spirit is slowly purifying.

Earthly wisdom has divided many churches. A power struggle between a pastor and an elder splintered a prospering church in our area. Lives were destroyed. The church was shattered, and the reputation of God was smeared. Here was the fruit of "disorder" and "evil practice" that James predicted would follow fallen wisdom.

Had the elder and pastor been willing to repent of their selfish ambition (pursuing the glory of God at their own expense), the conflict could have been resolved. This is because the wisdom that comes from heaven is peace loving. God's wisdom says, "He must become greater; I must become less" (John 3:30). It threatens no one. Therefore, its fruits are purity, peace, gentleness, considerateness, submissiveness, mercy, and sincerity (James 3:17).

How many homes have been destroyed by earthly wisdom? When husbands and wives pursue personal ambitions at the expense of their mates and children, they cannot build happy, unified families. I recently read the story of a well-known actress who married a successful actor. She worked the same long hours after her marriage, refusing to put her husband before her career, and their union failed. Earthly wisdom has its fruit.

Contrast this with the wisdom that permeated the marriage of Dr. Martyn Lloyd-Jones and his wife, Bethan, who was also a doctor. Shortly after their marriage, Martyn gave up a lucrative, promising career at an elite medical clinic that cared for the Queen of England and other influential patients. Instead, he preached the gospel in a poor industrial hamlet in rural Wales. He was ambitious, but it was unselfish ambition—focused on God's glory.

His wife, Bethan, also laid down a promising medical career to serve and follow her husband in the work to which God had called him. The nature of their wisdom appeared in their lives—and what glorious fruit it bore! The wisdom that characterized their union has greatly influenced the twentieth-century church.

John Stott carefully notes the choice that is always before us. "Powerless wisdom or foolish power: it was (and still is) a fateful choice. The one combination which is not an option is the wisdom of the world plus the power of God."[4]

Hidden in Christ

But maybe you need more proof that Charnock's definition was right. If so, there is none weightier than the cross.

133

Christ's crucifixion displayed Charnock's definition of heavenly wisdom in a way that surpasses words. It displays God's wisdom with action. At Jesus' death, absolute Goodness pursued his Father's glory at infinite personal expense. No hidden agendas and no selfish ambitions corrupted him. God's glory at his expense was Christ's determined goal, and the *means* with which he pursued it was an incomprehensible self-emptying death on a cross. That is why Paul wrote, "We preach Christ crucified . . . Christ the power of God and the *wisdom* of God" (I Cor. 1:23–24, emphasis mine).

Notice the contrast. Satan grasped for position, but Jesus completely emptied himself, not counting "equality with God something to be grasped" (Phil. 2:6). Jesus lowered himself an *infinite* distance in his self-abasement, incarnating himself in a poor, uneducated peasant family in the poorest region of Palestine—itself the least of nations. He did all this for his Father's glory. And this wisdom drove him to Golgotha. There he bore God's awful judgment for our sin, death by slow torture on a cross, in the process displaying both God's ends (his glory) and his means (death to self).

Therefore, the cross unlocked the third verse, Colossians 2:3: "Christ, in whom are hidden all the treasures of wisdom and knowledge." At the cross, I saw why God's wisdom was hidden and why it was a treasure.

God's wisdom was hidden because God's wisdom is unnatural to fallen man. In fact, the fallen mind despises God's wisdom. "The message of the cross is foolishness to those who are perishing," noted Paul (I Cor. 1:18). And, "We preach Christ crucified . . . foolishness to Gentiles" (I Cor. 1:23). I have lived in this foolishness, and so have you. That is one reason why twelve years passed before I was able to grasp the radical nature of God's wisdom. Even then, the transformation occurred strictly by God's mercy.

So the cross unlocks God's wisdom. And, oh, what wisdom! To those equipped by God to see and hear, the cross displays "Christ the power of God and the wisdom of God" (1 Cor. 1:24).

The cross also showed me why God's wisdom is a treasure. There I began to taste and experience the beauty of it. God's wisdom displays his incredible goodness and meekness. Who would not run to a God like this? Who would not want to own this wisdom for themselves?

In summary, to the degree that we really understand and practice the message of the cross, the pursuit of God's glory at his Son's expense, we are wise with God's wisdom. As James noted, these believers sow seeds of peace and reap a harvest of righteousness. You and I desperately need a greater measure of this wisdom.

Let's apply the thesis of this chapter to daily life. I want to note five important applications.

Wisdom Literature

First, the cross is the key to the wisdom literature of the Old Testament. For years I read a chapter of Proverbs and a Psalm daily, but I was slow to connect the wisdom of Psalms and Proverbs with the wisdom of the cross.

For example, Proverbs 9:10 reads, "The fear of the LORD is the beginning of wisdom." For many years this text bewildered me. I could not see the connection between the fear of God and wisdom. Not until I saw God's wisdom displayed at the cross did I begin to understand.

Those who understand the cross increasingly see their sin as God does, and therefore begin to *feel* about sin as does God. We begin to mourn for and hate it. In other words, at the cross God becomes larger and we become smaller. This separation is at the heart of the fear of God.

This "fear" opens God's wisdom to us because only in the light of God's immensity can I see the importance of living for the right end, his glory. And only in the light of my smallness can I feel overawed by the means he used to save me, his cross.

In other words, the fear that proceeds from the profound knowledge of God and man revealed at the cross is the key to the comprehension of heavenly wisdom. At the cross God opens the many-faceted splendors of his wisdom to us. Speaking of this process J. I. Packer notes:

> Not till we have become humble and teachable, standing in awe of God's holiness and sovereignty ("the great and awesome God," Neh. 1:5; compare 4:14; 9:32; Deut. 7:21; 10:17; Ps. 99:3; Jer. 20:11), acknowledging our own littleness, distrusting our own thoughts and willing to have our minds turned upside down, can divine wisdom become ours.[5]

The cross makes us humble and teachable. The cross puts us in awe of God's holiness and sovereignty. The cross reduces us in our own eyes.

The cross also illuminates passages like "Meaningless! Meaningless! . . . Utterly meaningless! Everything is meaningless" (Eccles. 1:1). It shows us the futility of temporal life apart from a relationship with Jesus Christ. On the cross Jesus bore the awful judgment that this world deserves. And that is exactly where life without Christ is headed—judgment. In summary, the cross is the necessary template through which we understand the wisdom literature in the Old Testament.

▰ Ends and Means

A second application is also very important. If God's wisdom pursues the perfect end with the perfect means, then every compromise of God's means to pursue a desirable end is a degradation of God's wisdom. This is true even for secondary ends like building families or civilizations. For example, Barna Research notes that both parents and churches want to reach children with the gospel, and they both agree that God has assigned this responsibility to parents. A good end. Barna notes that this is "an opportunity for churches to prepare parents for a more significant role in the spiritual development of their children."[6] However, his research found that although most churches offer many classes and programs for the children, "they do relatively little to equip parents to be effective spiritual guides."[7] But parents are God's ordained *means* for the spiritual development of children. When we inadvertently put the church in this role we corrupt God's means and therefore his wisdom.

Political activism can also sometimes compromise God's means. When we attempt to transform society through political reformation, we pursue a good end (a moral society) with a wrong means (politics). The right means is the proclamation of the gospel. We want to subject civilization to the authority of King Jesus. But the God-ordained *means* to this end is the proclamation of the gospel until God transforms so many individual hearts that society itself is slowly changed. God wants us to take our political responsibilities very seriously without trusting in politics for social salvation.

Understanding God's wisdom is also important because it saves us from pragmatism. Pragmatism is the idea that whatever works is right. In other words, the ends justify the means. For example, if modern business management and marketing principles help us reach the lost, they must be good. If psychology helps people feel better about themselves, we should recommend it. But the wisdom that appeared at the cross speaks otherwise. The means matter greatly to God, whether they get results or not. The proclamation of the law, our sinfulness, God's holiness, and justification by faith alone, rather than contemporary business marketing strategies, are the means that please God.[8] God is only glorified when we attain his ends with his means. To know his means we must be diligent students of the Bible. In the long run, God does not bless what is not built with his wisdom.

▆ *God's Building Tool*

The cross reminds us that wisdom is God's great building tool. It is to the Holy Spirit what a hammer is to a carpenter. "By wisdom the LORD laid the earth's foundations, by understanding he set the heavens in place" (Prov. 3:19). In the same way, wise Christians build their families with it. "The wise woman builds her house, but with her own hands the foolish one tears hers down" (Prov. 14:1). Pastors build churches with it. "By wisdom a house is built, and through understanding it is established; through knowledge its rooms are filled with rare and beautiful treasures" (Prov. 24:3–4).

As we have seen, God's wisdom unifies. Social organizations built with it grow in peace and grace. On the other hand, earthly wisdom sunders and fragments. A friend married a woman who proved to be contentious. She was out of control. (It got so bad that one day she assaulted the UPS delivery man.) How could he apply God's wisdom to his marriage? He decided to set aside every Tuesday to pray and fast for his wife, himself, and his marriage. He continued in this ministry for over fifteen years. Slowly his wife began to change, and so did he. Twenty-five years later their home was a sanctuary of peace. He pursued God's glory with the heart of a servant. He built his house with God's wisdom.

Think of all the people who place their careers before their family. Selfish ambition (earthly wisdom) is usually the motive, and domestic disintegration is usually the result.

We also can build sound businesses with God's wisdom. When one worker, to obtain promotion, slanders a competitor to his

138

boss, devilish wisdom is at work. Don't build with this wisdom. Any business fortunate enough to have employees salted with God's wisdom will prosper as each worker pursues the company's good even at his or her own expense.

A Christian was sharing with me how he determined to apply God's wisdom at work. "For the last few years," he said, "whenever my supervisor has set my annual sales goals, I have attempted to double them. I have not always succeeded, but I have always exceeded his goals, and I have enjoyed the satisfaction of serving my employer."

Wise Christian leaders also build with God's wisdom. As we have seen, earthly wisdom fuels many church splits. But leaders with God's wisdom serve unselfishly, and they surround themselves with unselfish people. As in the business world, God's wisdom unites congregations and builds up God's people.

Wisdom Proclaimed

The power of God inhabits the proclamation of his wisdom because the proclamation of God's wisdom is always the proclamation of the cross. If the lost are to be reached and saved, the wisdom of the cross must once again be unfurled against the banner of secularism. Paul understood that this was the base of his power. "But we preach Christ crucified . . . Christ, the *power* of God and the *wisdom* of God" (I Cor. 1:23–24, emphasis mine).

The power of God cannot be separated from the proclamation of the wisdom of God, and we desperately need that power in the church today. With this in mind, James Denney wrote, "On the rediscovery and fresh appreciation of it [the cross] the future and *power* of Christianity depend."[9] For this reason the message of the cross was always front and center in Paul's thinking. John Stott notes: "Paul's whole world was in orbit around the cross. It filled his vision, illumined his life, warmed his spirit. He 'gloried' in it. It meant more to him than anything else. Our perspective should be the same."[10]

Pray with me that God will raise up laborers to work in the harvest, believers filled with unselfish boldness, believers who understand the cross and its wisdom, believers willing to suffer and even die for the wisdom displayed there.

■ *Wisdom Displayed*

Our fifth application is exciting, and a fitting one upon which to conclude this chapter. God's eternal intention is that "now, through the church, the manifold wisdom of God should be made known to the rulers and authorities in the heavenly realms" (Eph. 3:10). What a glorious hope and responsibility. Who can comprehend a future so glorious? The church will ultimately display God's cross wisdom to the principalities and authorities looking down from heavenly realms.

This means we have a responsibility to internalize God's wisdom. A people saturated in God's wisdom are obsessed with the glory of God, and they are willing to lose their lives to advance it. The church has displayed this wisdom for brief moments in history.

The Moravians, the first Protestant missionaries in modern history, marched forth from Germany in the 1730s to evangelize the world. They had been transformed at their little compound, known simply as Herrnhut, by a great inundation of the Holy Spirit. Their passion was the glory of God through the conversion of souls, and they paid a tremendous price for their zeal. Many experienced bitter persecution. Others died at the hands of their persecutors, but God was glorified, and when all was said and done, that was enough for these courageous soldiers. They lived and displayed the wisdom of God. So does every church that lives in the shadow of the cross.

Conclusion

The Bible gives us at least three tips on how to acquire God's wisdom. First, confess that you have no wisdom in yourself. As we saw, God is the fount of all wisdom. "To the *only wise God* be glory forever through Jesus Christ" (Rom. 16:27, emphasis mine). We enter the world bound by Satan's wisdom. We need grace and help to be transformed by God's.

Second, don't be bashful. Ask. God is a gracious giver. "If any of you lacks wisdom, he should ask God, who gives generously to all without finding fault, and it will be given to him" (James 1:5). I asked in 1973, and God was faithful. The answer didn't come when I wanted, but come it did, and it radically changed my life and perspective.

Third, learn to fear God. We have already noted that "the fear of the LORD is the beginning of wisdom" (Prov. 9:10). Three is God's number of exclamation, and since the Bible repeats this verse exactly three times (also see Job 28:28; Ps. 111:10), it must be an important concept. Meditate on it. Ask for God's light. Ask him to teach you to fear him. There is little heavenly wisdom where there is little fear of God.

We fear God to the degree that God is big and we are small in our own eyes. In many ways, humility is a synonym for the fear of God. The bigger God looms, the more we love him and pursue his glory from the posture of a servant. "The fear of the LORD is a fountain of life" (Prov. 14:27). Drink liberally from this stream.

In summary, contrary to popular opinion, we do not gain God's wisdom from experience. It does not accrue to us with age. (Spurgeon, Whitefield, and Robert McCheyne obtained it in their early twenties.) It has nothing to do with cleverness or gray beards. No, God reveals his wisdom to those who fear him and ask with expectant hearts. The Holy Spirit reveals it at the cross, and it comes as we increasingly see and understand the cross—as we increasingly perceive the incredibly good, self-emptying, gracious God who died there on our behalf.

We recognize its authenticity by its fruits.

What I know of God's wisdom has become my valued treasure. It came in answer to prayer, and it came as I humbled myself before God, learning to fear him. In the same way, may the discovery and practice of God's wisdom be the unearthing of hidden treasure for you.

10

The Supreme Sufferer
in the Universe

"Evil will come of that evil, but it is still a long way off, and I will see to it the worst falls upon myself. . . . As Adam's race has done the harm, Adam's race shall help to heal it."

Aslan speaking of the entrance of sin into Narnia, from C. S. Lewis's *The Magician's Nephew*

We had been eagerly waiting for nine months, and at last our first child was to be born. Judy and I were excited and entered the hospital with high hopes. We had gone through child-birthing classes, and I had learned how to "coach" Judy. The teachers told us that the average first labor took twelve hours, that it was usually a joyful event, and that some women "didn't even feel pain." My wife's labor, however, did not fit into this tidy box of happy expectations.

Twenty hours after checking into the hospital, Judy was still suffering strong back labor. Her pain was excruciating and had been since the beginning. The agony of her suffering was eating me up. I lifted my eyes to heaven and cried out, "Lord, you love Judy more than I do. Please bring this child into the world and end my beloved's pain. I can't bear to watch her suffer anymore." But there was no answer. Heaven was silent. Finally, after twenty-four hours of hard labor, our daughter Sarah, bruised and battered by forceps, entered the world.

This experience was my first contact with real suffering, and it was an eye-opener. How could a loving God allow my wife to suffer this way?

If you have lived long enough, you know that suffering is a part of life in a fallen world. From minor headaches to the liquidation of civilizations, suffering is all around us. The Saint Bartholomew's Day Massacre in 1572 is a good example.

God launched the Protestant Reformation in 1517 through the ministry of Martin Luther. Within a generation thousands were being converted to Protestantism in Roman Catholic France. Their enemies nicknamed the Protestants "Huguenots." It is estimated that by 1562 there were two million French Protestants and about 1,250 Reformed churches in France. Then in August of 1572, on Saint Bartholomew's Day, the pro-Catholic government turned on the Huguenots, loosing an explosion of popular hatred. God's people suffered greatly.

> In the terrible days that followed some 3,000 Huguenots were killed in Paris, and perhaps another 8,000 in other provincial cities. . . . Mobs attacked Protestants in their homes, indiscriminately slaughtering men, women, and children. Victims were stabbed, shot, or beaten to death; their bloodied bodies were often dismembered, dragged through the streets, and thrown into the Seine. Vigilante bands searched for suspected Protestants and looted their homes and shops.[1]

This kind of misery always elicits the question, Why do bad things happen to good people? But the agony of the Huguenots is just the tip of the iceberg of human suffering. As I write, congestive heart failure is slowly constricting the life of my mother-in-law, and a friend's twenty-nine-year-old daughter is dying of complications from diabetes. Last year I helplessly watched three close friends suffer acute clinical depression. They were emotionally burnt out, hopeless, and suicidal. They have all recovered, but while in depression's grip, the emotional pain and trauma were severe. The problem with these examples of suffering is that they often shake our confidence in God.

The Problem of Evil

The existence of suffering, sin, and pain presents a basic theological problem. I came to grips with it over lunch with a non-Christian friend. He knew all about Christianity; he had many Christian relatives but had personally rejected the faith. I screwed up my courage to talk to him about it.

"Mike, what keeps you from becoming a Christian?" I asked.

He looked at me thoughtfully. "Do you believe that God is love?"

"Yes."

"Do you believe that God is sovereign, in control of everything?"

"Of course," I answered, wondering where he was going.

"That's my problem," he said. "Everywhere I look, people are hurting, suffering, in pain. Starvation stalks the poor of Southeast Asia. Cancer devastates the rich in America. Hurt is everywhere. Therefore, God can't be both loving and sovereign. He must be sovereign but not loving, and that's why pain exists. Or he must want to end suffering, because he is loving, but cannot, because he is not sovereign and that's why the suffering continues. But he can't be both. In either case I can't worship a half-God."

145

I was so surprised by the depth of his answer that I was unable to give him a satisfactory response. He had just given me a classic statement of the problem of evil. It sent me to the Bible for answers, and I found them at the cross.

Mike understood the Bible. Despite the evil and sin around us, it clearly teaches that God is love, and that he is also absolutely sovereign. In fact, the Bible teaches that God is so sovereign that every event in the cosmos is inexorably working toward his predetermined end, according to his perfect plan. At the same time, it declares that we are moral agents responsible for our decisions. Although God does not will evil, he has allowed it. Although God does not force us to do anything, he is in absolute control of all human decisions. Beyond these truths we cannot go.

How can we reconcile these seeming contradictions? How can God be sovereign and we be free moral agents at the same time? How can a sovereign God allow suffering and still be good? Logically, within the context of finite human understanding, these problems can't be resolved.

However, the absence of a completely satisfactory solution will not trouble those who accept God's infinity. If God is infinite and we are finite, there should be vast areas of knowledge completely hidden from us. In fact, it is arrogance to presume that finite minds should be able to resolve these problems. Ultimately, faith just bows in solemn reverence to God's omniscient goodness and says, "Yes, Lord."

Why good people suffer is the question asked by the Book of Job. God does not give Job and his friends the answer they want. Basically, he tells them to mind their own business. The book starts with Job questioning God and ends with God questioning Job. Job concludes, "I despise myself and repent in dust and ashes" (Job 42:6). As Job discovers, we, rather than God, are the problem.

When God created the universe, he did not intend this suffering. He inflicted it because we rebelled, and he is just. In fact, he hates death. It reminds him of our rebellion and all the suffering that has followed. But his cross and resurrection will someday ultimately defeat death (1 Cor. 15:25–26).

The cross speaks to the problem of evil. It doesn't explain how evil can exist in the presence of infinite goodness and sovereignty. But there, on the cross, God participated in the pain caused by evil—a truth infinitely more valuable. As Paul Billheimer noted, "The infinitely happy God is the supreme Sufferer in the universe."[2] The cross speaks this important message. In fact, the cross speaks three life-changing lessons about suffering.

1. The cross tells us that suffering, sin, and evil highlight, enhance, and glorify the goodness of God.
2. The cross reminds us that God is absolutely sovereign over all suffering, and he uses it all for our good.
3. The cross proves and demonstrates God's great compassion.

As C. S. Lewis so eloquently wrote, "The world is a dance in which good, descending from God, is disturbed by evil arising from the creatures, and the resulting conflict is resolved by God's own assumption of the suffering nature which evil produces."[3] The wonderful truth is that suffering, pain, and evil have all redounded for our good and God's glory *because* God's Son took upon himself the suffering that our sin deserves.

God Uses Evil for His Glory

God uses evil to glorify his goodness. The existence of sin and evil amplifies the moral beauty of God. This is the first truth the cross speaks about suffering.

I drove through town with my high beams on at noon, but no one "flashed" or honked or even seemed annoyed. Why? It was broad daylight. They could barely see my headlights. But in the dead of a moonless night, even low beams irritate oncoming traffic. We discern light in the presence of its opposite, darkness. So it is with virtue.

So when angels and humans chose to rebel, God determined to use evil for good. This is what Augustine meant when he wrote, "God judged it better to bring good out of evil than to suffer no evil at all." In other words, God deemed it better to give us freedom to sin, knowing that he could use evil, if we fell, to magnify his glory, than to deny us the moral freedom that would risk the possibility of sin.

Suffering for enemies speaks louder than suffering for friends. God would be no less loving had he died for good people, but when he went to the cross for the wicked, for his enemies, for those deserving wrath not love, his goodness erupted with infinite beauty. The sinfulness and unworthiness of those for whom he died revealed the depth of his awesome love.

I made an appointment to meet a friend for lunch and then promptly forgot. I felt terrible. I called, and he graciously forgave me. Imagine, though, that he had just forgiven another friend who had raped his wife, murdered his children, and burnt his house to the ground. Which forgiveness would be greater? Which forgiveness would speak most loudly about this man's goodness? The latter. The more unworthy the beloved, the greater the love displayed. In the same way, God has used sin to magnify his love and our joy in beholding it.

Our sin does not make the love of God greater. Nothing can be added to it or taken from it. It is perfect and always will be. However, humanity's sin enhances our power to discern a love that would otherwise be hidden from us.

In other words, God has taken the sin and rebellion that the devil meant for harm and transformed it into a vehicle for the demonstration of his goodness. The cross is the apex of this process. We saw in chapters 3 and 4 that God could not reconcile us to himself without suffering sin's penalty in our place. But God so loved the world that he was willing to endure infinite suffering for our happiness. As the old hymn goes, "What wondrous love is this, O my soul, O my soul?" Therefore, evil, pain, and suffering have enhanced the brilliance of the light of God's infinite love in a dark and fallen universe.

For example, mercy and grace depend upon the existence of evil for definition. "Amazing grace, how sweet the sound" would be incomprehensible without sin in a fallen world. Why? Because by definition mercy is the relaxation of *deserved* punishment. Without sin there would be no punishment to relax. In the same way, grace is *unmerited* favor. It is reward given to those who deserve punishment. Without sin and its deserved judgment, we would not be able to comprehend the riches of God's mercy or grace. The terms would have no meaning for us.

In fact, the cross is the only rational argument for the problem of evil advanced by any major religion. Neither Buddha, Krishna, Allah, nor any other god has participated in human suffering. They stand above, aloof, and apart from the human dilemma. They offer no explanation for suffering and therefore provide no basis for compassion.

By contrast, Jesus Christ became one with us and suffered with us. In fact, he suffered in a way that a mere creature cannot comprehend. He endured an infinite punishment. He suffered emotional and spiritual torments on the cross of which we have no knowledge. By so doing he sanctified suffering and pain. He hasn't taken them away, but the cross says, "Pain has purpose. To prove this I have participated redemptively with you in the hurt of a fallen world."

Hallelujah! What wonderful news for the hurting.

Not only does sin and suffering provide a context in which to appreciate mercy and grace, but these things also amplify God's love. We measure love by its cost. God's love is an ardent, impassioned desire for our happiness. It is greater than affection. It is not a feeling but a decision to act on behalf of another despite the cost. Had sin caused no pain and suffering, necessitating a costly redemption, God's love would have no tangible, visible cost. We would have no way to measure it.

The presence of evil not only glorifies God's mercy, grace, and love, but it also displays God's justice and his hatred of evil (Rom. 9:22). God hates evil, and our suffering constantly reminds us of this truth. God has used evil to display the perfections of his just judgments. For just one sin, not many, God judged the entire universe. Because of sin, men labor in pain and stress to support their families (Gen. 3:17–18). Because of sin, women birth children in pain and suffering (Gen. 3:16). Because of sin, nations war against one another and races persecute each other. These pains and travails point us to the perfections of God's judgments and his hatred of evil.

In summary, evil unveils the love, mercy, and grace of God in a way that a virtuous, painless environment would not. God did not will sin or suffering, but he has decided to use it for good.

God Uses Evil for Our Good

The cross speaks a second important message about pain and suffering. God *always* uses it for our good. "In all things [especially pain and suffering] God works for the good of those who love him, who have been called according to his purpose" (Rom. 8:28). As the old saying goes, "No pressure, no diamonds." C. S. Lewis has aptly observed, "God whispers to us in our pleasures, speaks in our conscience, but shouts in our pains. It is his megaphone to arouse a deaf world."[4]

Bob fell behind on his taxes. Over a period of several years the debt grew into an insurmountable mountain. He hid these problems from his wife, Anne, all the while spiraling deeper and deeper into hopeless, vicious depression. Finally, he took his own life, leaving his widow huge debts and no life insurance or cash assets.

A few days later, in the midst of her shock and grief, the IRS knocked on the door, explaining her husband's debt and looking for payment. The stress and pain of facing her husband's suicide and then her overwhelming debt was almost unbearable. Anne cried out to God, placing her faith in him. He miraculously provided protection from the IRS and brought her through this terrible time.

Ten years later she told me, "I pray every day that I will never forget the lessons God taught me during that dark time. I would never ask to go through it again, but I would never take back the deepening of my relationship with God that occurred through that pain either." She had learned from experience the truth that God is sovereign over evil, and that he always uses it for the good of those who trust him. This is what William Gurnall meant when he wrote, "God's wounds cure, but sin's kisses kill."[5] God has turned evil upside down, using it all for good.

God took another dear friend's business from the heights of success to the depths of bankruptcy in eighteen months. He became deeply depressed, often waking in the middle of the night with panic attacks. He had to be medicated. Then his health failed, and he went through three major intestinal surgeries. To top it all off, his father-in-law, with whom he was very close, developed Alzheimer's. My friend was in God's furnace of affliction.

But when it was all over he told me, "I am a new person. I will never be the same. My suffering has transformed my spiritual life and my relationship with God."

In each of these situations God demonstrated his mastery of human suffering. No problem can touch you or me without God's permission. And if it does, it will all be ordered and orchestrated for God's glory and our good. What wonderful news! We can endure anything if we really believe this.

This does not mean that God is responsible for pain. Stress, sorrow, grief, worry, physical pain all have their origins in sin—not necessarily the personal sin of the sufferer, but the sin of humankind in general. (Pain can also be the byproduct of personal rebellion.) But in either case, God is so big that he can give us moral freedom, and when we use that freedom for evil, he can use the consequent pain for our ultimate happiness and his glory. The life of Joseph illustrates this truth.

Joseph

Motivated by jealousy, Joseph's brothers sold him into slavery. Imagine Joseph's feelings of rejection and betrayal. After that, he served as a slave in the house of Potiphar for about five years. Then the slander of Potiphar's wife condemned him to an Egyptian prison for several years. Not until his suffering and rejection had ripened and matured him did he become the prime minister of Egypt, second only to Pharaoh.

Years later his brothers came to Egypt seeking grain. By now Joseph understood God's purpose for his suffering. Like my widowed friend, Joseph saw God working sovereignly through his pain. Without Joseph's grain his brothers would have starved and none of God's promises to Abraham and his descendants would have been fulfilled. "It was to save lives that God sent me ahead of you," he told the brothers who betrayed him. "*God sent me ahead of you* to preserve for you a remnant on earth and to save your lives by a great deliverance. So then, it was not you who sent me here, but God" (Gen. 45:7–8, emphasis mine).

God sent him? To the eye of unbelief, his brothers had sent him. But by faith Joseph saw how God had used his suffering to mature him and preserve his family. At once he perceived that

God was both good and in full control of his pain and suffering. Do you and I share Joseph's confidence? To the degree that we do, we can weather anything. The cross is the strongest statement of, and proof for, this truth.

The Cross

A few weeks after Jesus' death, Peter said, "This man was handed over to you by God's *set purpose and foreknowledge;* and you, with the help of wicked men, put him to death by nailing him to the cross" (Acts 2:23, emphasis mine).

Peter knew that from before the beginning of time God had purposed and planned his Son's suffering and death without violating the moral responsibility of those who murdered him. Jesus died according to "God's set purpose and foreknowledge." Every detail was in God's perfect timing and will. From Peter's threefold denial to the crown of thorns, God had it all under control. And yet the men who crucified him acted freely, motivated by their own wickedness. As with Joseph, God turned human sin on its head, using it to redeem millions.

Maybe you're wondering how God can be this sovereign and we can be responsible at the same time. You are not alone. No one can understand how both of these things can be true. It is accepted by faith. Since God is infinite in power and intelligence, there is no rational barrier to this marvelous fact. God planned his Son's death, fulfilling every ancient prophecy in precise detail. He did this to convince us in our own time of suffering that "in all things God works for the good of those who love him, who have been called according to his purpose" (Rom. 8:28).

He not only used it for our good, but he also used it for his glory. God used the cross to exalt Christ to the pinnacle of highest glory that every knee might bow and every tongue confess that Jesus Christ is Lord (Phil. 2:10–11). The cross proclaims loudly and clearly this central message: God is sovereign over all suffering. He is good, and he uses evil for the ultimate good of all who trust him. God was sovereign over the Saint Bartholomew's Day Massacre and my wife's painful labor. He used both for good.

God Is Compassionate

The cross speaks a third message to those suffering. It demonstrates God's great compassion, which is his capacity to empathize with someone who is hurting.

Compassion usually is not the first divine attribute we think of. Love comes to mind first. But God is, and always has been, infinitely compassionate. When God declared his glory to Moses, the first thing he said was, "The LORD, the LORD, the *compassionate* and gracious God" (Exod. 34:6, emphasis mine).

Although we need suffering to become more compassionate, Jesus does not. So if suffering did not make Christ more compassionate, what purpose, besides our redemption, did his suffering achieve? It convinces us of God's compassion, and if you are like me you often need convincing. It tells us he understands. It encourages us to go to him in our time of need. Why? Because Jesus clothed himself in human flesh and suffered with us.

Human words cannot express this mystery. Had he not died on a cross, his great compassion would have no context. We would have his word that he was compassionate, but no demonstration of it. But glory to God! He suffered with us, and for us, to turn us to him in our day of great stress and pain.

When oppressed by depression and rejection, when feeling like God is far away, look to the cross. The Son of God understands. Remember, on the cross he received what sin deserves. He was completely forsaken. "My God, my God, why have you forsaken me?" (Matt. 27:46). You have never felt forsaken or abandoned like Christ. He understands. He feels your pain. He is "compassionate and gracious."

When depression or sickness grip you, stealing your joy, when the pain is great and you feel like there is no hope or remedy, remember the cross. Evil men *tortured* Jesus to death. Every cell screamed with agony; stress strained every nerve to the breaking point. He felt hopeless. When I feel hopeless, and I have many times, I remember his cross compassion, and I run to him.

In the middle of my career I took a promotion into management. It was a time of great stress because I had responsibility without authority. The pressure was acute. I started waking up in the middle of the night, worried, stressed, fearful, and unable to sleep.

A few years later one of my teenage children went through a year of deep depression, fear, and hopelessness. Again, my nights were sleepless with worry and stress. I paced the floor in prayer, crying out to God for mercy. Although I knew I should have the "peace that passes understanding," I didn't.

But I could flee to Christ in my need. Why? Because of his cross; I knew Jesus understood. On the night before his crucifixion, he actually *sweat blood* (Luke 22:44). Now that is anxiety! That makes a panic attack seem like child's play. Because of the cross, I realized I didn't have to have my life together. I could turn to Jesus and confess my inadequacy, certain that he understood.

Never forget, God made Jesus perfect through suffering (Heb. 2:10). This does not mean that Jesus was sinful. The Greek word for perfect in these verses is *teleos,* from which we get our word *telescope.* It means "brought to the fullness of God's purpose and usefulness."

He also learned obedience through what he suffered (Heb. 5:8). Knowing this, we too can confidently approach God in our time of need. As C. S. Lewis noted, he "shouts to us" through our suffering. If God's perfect Son needed suffering to bring him into the fullness of God's purpose, how much more you and I?

Why Is This Important?

We can draw several lessons from what the Bible tells us about suffering.

First, life will not always be easy. Some teach that real faith brings a painless, wealthy, trouble-free life, and that pain or poverty are certain proofs of unbelief. But this message distorts God's truth, and the cross is the proof. Sometimes we do suffer because of unbelief, but at other times we suffer despite great faith. Of one thing you can be sure. You live in a fallen world, and you will encounter trouble. The question is not if, it is when. C. S. Lewis had a more biblical perspective: "We are not necessarily doubting that God will do the best for us; we are wondering how painful the best will turn out to be."

Second, God tries our faith so that we may try his faithfulness. Trouble, pain, and trial always test our confidence in God's goodness. *If God is really good, why is this happening to me?* we wonder. James calls this "the testing of your faith" (James 1:3). Trials do not usually test our faith in God's existence, they test our faith in his goodness. The irony is that, as we have seen, God uses pain and trouble to witness to his goodness. He suffered on a cross to glorify his goodness. So expect trouble to test your faith in his ultimate goodness. Endure it, looking to the cross, and in the end your suffering will increase your confidence that he means it all for good.

Third, suffering mixed with faith deepens our compassion, but suffering mixed with unbelief amplifies bitterness and despair. Pain is evil only to the degree that it conquers us. And without faith, it will conquer us. But God wants us to conquer sin, bitterness, and despair by trusting him in the day of pain, not running from it.

Have you ever noticed that some people grow happier and more content with age, while others become more cynical and bitter? It all depends on their reaction to suffering.

Beth lost her husband to brain cancer after many years of marriage. A few months later her eighteen-year-old son died in a head-on car accident. And then one of her grandchildren died of SIDS. This poor woman was devastated, but she clung to God by faith. She believed against all hope that God was good and that he was sovereign over evil. She increasingly thanked God for his sovereignty over her troubles and his goodness, and she emerged victorious from her grieving and misery. Today Beth is a woman of deep compassion.

Max was a Jewish friend who had emigrated from Poland in 1920. At age eighty-three he was dying of bone cancer. He saw no redemptive purpose in evil, pain, or suffering. For him life had become meaningless. He had seen much sorrow, but it had not produced compassion. I tried, unsuccessfully, to share the gospel with him, and a few months later I heard he had died bitter and resentful. Because he had no faith, he learned little compassion.

Fourth, if we really believe these three lessons taught by the cross, we need never fear future suffering. When accidents, cancer, or bankruptcy happen to those we know, we are tempted to ask, What if it happens to me? Then we waste a lot of time fearing future suffering.

Christians should anticipate future suffering without fear. Why? Because that is how Jesus approached suffering. "For the joy set before him [Jesus] endured the cross" (Heb. 12:2). If we really believe that God brings good out of suffering, that God expresses his love through suffering, and that God empowers us to endure suffering, we will never fear the future. "Our light and momentary troubles are achieving for us an eternal glory that far outweighs them all" (2 Cor. 4:17), wrote one who knew about suffering firsthand.[6] Do we really believe this verse, or is it just words? Fear of the future cannot control those who stand on this truth.

Fifth, God's love depends upon suffering for its perfection. Paul Billheimer noted the truth that "there is no love without self-giving. There is no self-giving without pain. Therefore, there is no love (agape love) without suffering. Suffering is an essential ingredient of agape love and therefore of a moral universe."[7]

We can exercise affection without pain, but we cannot practice agape love until we push through pain for the happiness of another. An ardent, impassioned desire for the happiness of a grouchy husband is greater agape than that for an emotionally stable, cheerful husband. The first is very costly, the second almost costless. An ardent, impassioned desire for the happiness of an adulterous wife is greater than that for a nurturing, faithful wife. The cost defines the love. The love of God would have no measurable cost in a world without sin and suffering.

John Huss's terrible sufferings for Christ in 1415 gave him an opportunity to demonstrate the depth of his love for God. After six months' imprisonment, during most of which time he was chained to a wall in a cold, wet, subterranean cell, he was brutally interrogated by the church council for his stand on the Bible. Toward the end of it all, he returned to his cell complaining of a violent headache, constant vomiting, gallstones, and painful toothache. The council burnt him at the stake a few days later.[8] The measure of Huss's willingness to persevere through suffering was the measure of his love for God.

Conclusion

We have noted that God did not will sin and suffering but that he uses it for our good. Had Adam not sinned there would have been no pain and suffering. And we have seen that without pain and suffering, we would have no capacity to imitate God's love. The evil of pain and suffering in a fallen world provides us this opportunity. Therefore, in mercy God has used Adam's sin to actually amplify his capacity to reward Adam's undeserving posterity. In our fallen world we must fight through pain and adversity to love. Therefore, our love is greater than it would have been in a perfect world, and our reward will be greater! Behold the mercy and grace of God.

We began this chapter with the problem of evil—the problem that sin presents to the mind of unbelief. We have seen how the cross speaks to this problem. Peter Kreeft sums it up well: "Suffering is the evidence against God, the reason not to trust him. Jesus [and his cross] is the evidence for God, the reason to trust Him."[9] My prayer is that God opens the eye of your heart to this truth and that it strengthens you to stand in the evil day.

159

11

The Heart of Worship

God is not impressed with our worship on Sunday morning
at church if we are practicing "cruise-control" obedience
the rest of the week. You may sing with reverent zest or
great emotional fervor, but your worship is only as pleasing
to God as the obedience that accompanies it.

Jerry Bridges

Fights over the style of worship (hymns or choruses), the instruments used (organs or guitars), or the outward manifestations (raising or folding of hands) have stressed many congregations. We laugh and call them worship wars, but something is radically wrong with our concept of worship when congregations become obsessed with these minor issues.

In addition, many people, especially the youth, choose churches based on the quality of the music rather than the truth proclaimed from the pulpit. When asked why they pick a particular church, most of my young friends cite worship music as the leading factor. In fact, many churches have discovered that performance-quality worship music will make a church grow faster than anything else. Clearly something is wrong with our understanding of worship!

There seems to be little correlation between our expression of worship on Sunday morning and our fruitfulness. Sometimes those with the most flamboyant outward expressions of worship have proven most superficial in their daily walk, while those with the dullest outward expressions of worship have been most fruitful.

A friend told me about two men with whom he enthusiastically worshipped with shouts of joy and raised hands for many weeks. But when he found out they were addicted to pornography, he confronted them in love. Rather than expressing sorrow and repentance, they became angry and defensive.

On the other hand, I know Christians who sing three-hundred-year-old hymns from musty hymnals to out-of-sync organ music who love their spouses, pay their bills, raise godly, disciplined children, and give extravagantly to Christ and his kingdom.

John 4:23

The Bible is a noisy book. Raised hands,[1] clapping,[2] dancing,[3] even shouting,[4] can be defended from Scripture, and these are all appropriate in the right context, but I am convinced that worship is something deeper and more substantial than these outward expressions.

Jesus made this profound statement to the Samaritan woman: "Yet a time is coming and has now come when the true worshippers will worship the Father in spirit and truth, for they are the kind of worshippers the Father seeks. God is spirit, and his worshippers must worship in spirit and in truth" (John 4:23–24).

I wanted to be the kind of worshipper the Father seeks. So I set out to discover what Jesus meant by "worship in spirit and in truth."

My search ended at the cross!

What Worship in Spirit and Truth Is Not

Worship in "spirit and truth" is not something outward; it is not singing and music. You can sing hymns or choruses, experiencing great emotional uplifts, and not worship in spirit and truth. On the other hand you can sing four hymns a cappella and sit down, having felt little, but worship God deeply in spirit and truth. True worship affects our emotions, but it is deeper than feelings.

Although corporate singing on Sunday morning can express this worship, singing is not the main idea. Did you know that the English New Testament uses the word *worship* over eighty times, but it rarely does so in the context of music or singing? Behind the scriptural concept of worship is something more profound than corporate vocals.

The same truth applies to prayers and intercessions. We often call these worship, and they can be, but you can do either in "flesh and in falsehood" or in "spirit and in truth."

We also use the word *worship* for church attendance. "I didn't see you at worship Sunday," we might note to a friend. But you can occupy a church pew all of your life and never worship in spirit and truth.

In fact, all of the above done in flesh and falsehood merely amplify God's displeasure toward us. The net effect becomes counterproductive. In fact, what I think is building a bridge between myself and God—worship—can actually be separating me from him.

God abhors worship in flesh and falsehood, and we have all practiced it.

163

Worship That Offends God

This was the problem of ancient Israel, and we can learn from their plight. In the first six chapters of Leviticus, God gave them elaborate instructions on how he wanted to be worshipped. But five hundred years later, something had gone wrong.

> "The multitude of your sacrifices—
>   what are they to me?" says the LORD.   .
> "I have more than enough of burnt offerings,
>   of rams and the fat of fattened animals;
> I have no pleasure
>   in the blood of bulls and lambs and goats.
> When you come to appear before me,
>   who has asked this of you,
>   this trampling of my courts?
>   [Insert singing, prayers, church attendance.]
> Stop bringing meaningless offerings!"
>
> Isaiah 1:11–13

It was not the sacrifices that were wrong; after all, God had commanded them. The problem was this: Israel offered the animals while withholding their hearts and lives from God. This, despite the fact that the burnt offering was supposed to be an outward sign of the worshipper's life consumed, like the animal, in service to God. Instead, Israel gave God the outward sign while keeping their lives to themselves. They made the fatal mistake of assuming worship was something external, something outward. They worshipped God on their terms, not his, and they bought the deceit that God was happy with this arrangement.

In short, they did not worship in spirit and truth. And we can do the same thing with the sacrifices of corporate singing, tithing, prayers, or church attendance. You can make a great outward sacrifice to God, but if it does not express a heart consecrated to him, it is worship in flesh and falsehood.

This is what Samuel meant when he said to Saul, "Does the LORD delight in burnt offerings and sacrifices as much as in obeying the voice of the LORD? To obey is better than sacrifice, and to heed is better than the fat of rams" (1 Sam. 15:22). It is what Jesus meant when he told the Pharisees, "These people honor me with their lips, but their hearts are far from me. They worship me in vain; their teachings are but rules taught by men" (Matt. 15:8–9).

Worship in Spirit

Few subjects have been disputed as much as the definition of what it means to worship in spirit and in truth. Stephen Charnock, the eminent Puritan scholar, devoted over seventy pages to its definition in his epochal book *The Existence and Attributes of God.*[5]

The definition is important! If your boss announced that he would promote anyone who gave him enebriomalgia, you would immediately look up the definition of this term so that you could give it to him.[6] Well, Jesus said, those who worship "in spirit and truth . . . are the kind of worshippers the Father seeks" (John 4:23). So let us vigorously pursue this definition. First, we will define what it means to worship God in spirit.

Worship in spirit is worship enjoyed by those who are spiritual, i.e., born of God. New Birth involves a transformation, and at New Birth a fleshly person becomes spiritual. "I tell you the truth, no one can enter the kingdom of God unless he is born of water and the Spirit," exclaimed Jesus. "Flesh gives birth to flesh, but the Spirit gives birth to spirit" (John 3:5–6).

Those born again have been resurrected from death to life— from a life in the flesh to a life lived in the Spirit. The first sign of this "life" is that God begins to communicate with them. That is

165

why Jesus said, "The Spirit gives life; the flesh counts for nothing. The words I have spoken to you *are spirit and they are life*" (John 6:63, emphasis mine). And that is why Paul wrote, "The man without the Spirit [the man in the flesh] does not accept the things that come from the Spirit of God, for they are foolishness to him, and he cannot understand them, because they are spiritually discerned" (1 Cor. 2:14). Those who are spiritual hear from God.

This matters because all true worship is a response to God's revelation. God initiates worship by speaking to us, and we must be "spiritual" to hear from him. Worship is not something that we fabricate or produce. God reveals some aspect of his moral beauty—his love, mercy, or holiness—and we respond with worship. In other words, to the degree that God communicates his proper nature to us we respond with worship. "Worship is dialogical," notes Michael Horton. "God speaks and we respond."[7]

Second, worship in spirit means without material form. The emphasis is on, "*God is spirit*, and his worshippers must worship in spirit and in truth" (John 4:24, emphasis mine). The first commandment prohibited the worship of false gods, but the second commandment tells us *how* to worship the true God. "You shall not make for yourself an idol, or any likeness of what is in heaven above or on the earth beneath or in the water under the earth. You shall not worship them or serve them; for I, the LORD your God, am a jealous God" (Exod. 20:4–5 NASB). Jesus had the second commandment in mind when he said, "God is Spirit."

Because God is infinite in power, knowledge, and presence, he must be a spirit. Everything material is finite, therefore an infinite God cannot be material. For this reason it is a monumental insult to worship God in any material form—using statues or pictures to represent him. By doing this we say, "God is not infinite. He is finite." That is why the language of the second commandment is so strong. It protects the glory of God's infinity.

You say, "Thank goodness I have never bowed down to a statue or picture of God." But we don't get off the hook that easy. This commandment also prohibits mental impressions of God that are unworthy of him. Have you rejected the wrath of God? Have you entertained the idea that God tolerates sin?[8] Have you read Romans 9 and recoiled in disgust? Have you flirted with the idea that God does not know the future or that he is not sovereign? Then you have worshipped God in flesh, not spirit.

In summary, only those born of God can worship in spirit. This worship is a response to God's self-disclosure; it is the worship of God without material form and with thoughts worthy of him.

Worship in Truth

What does it mean to worship God in truth? First, those who worship God in truth give him the sacrifice he wants. We noted how Israel sacrificed bulls and goats when God wanted their hearts, their very lives.

We sometimes do the same. We worship God with exuberant corporate singing, raised hands (if you are from a charismatic background), tithes, or regular church attendance, but withhold what he really wants—the fabric of our daily lives given in his service. When we do so, we worship in falsehood.

The Old Testament repeatedly describes the worship that God seeks.

With what shall I come to the LORD and bow myself before the God on high? Shall I come to Him with burnt offerings, with yearling calves? . . . He has told you, O man, what is good; and what does the LORD require of you but to do justice, to love kindness, and to walk humbly with your God?

Micah 6:6, 8 NASB

167

The psalmist reminds us that spiritual worship is a broken and contrite spirit. "The sacrifices of God are a broken spirit; a broken and a contrite heart, O God, you will not despise" (Ps. 51:17). Are you broken by sin, contrite over your failings? Do you see sin and evil as God does? Do you fear God? Do you tremble at his Word? This worship is rare in the modern church. It requires the knowledge of sin. The cross highlights our sinfulness. Therefore, this worship is a fruit of cross-centered living.

We also worship in truth when we offer the sacrifice of thanksgiving in our time of need and disappointment. "I am in pain and distress; may your salvation, O God, protect me. I will praise God's name in song and glorify him with thanksgiving. This will please the LORD more than an ox, more than a bull with its horns and hoofs" (Ps. 69:29–31).

Oh, how difficult to thank God while lying on your back in the bottom of life's ditch. In 1758, Princeton College called Jonathan Edwards to be their next president. Jonathan went ahead of his wife, Sarah, to begin the new job while she stayed home to pack and wrap up the loose ends. In the interim Jonathan died. A note came by courier explaining the tragic facts. Sarah was devastated. They had been married for more than thirty years and were deeply in love and extremely dependent on each other.

Left alone with a brood of children to raise and suffering from rheumatism so badly that she could barely write, Sarah scratched out this note to her grown daughter Esther. "What shall I say? A holy and good God has covered us with a dark cloud. O that we may kiss the rod, and lay our hands on our mouths! The Lord has done it. He has made me adore his goodness, that we had him [Jonathan] so long. But my God lives; and he has my heart. . . . We are all given to God; and there I am, and love to be."[9]

These are the words of one who worships in spirit and truth.

In summary, worship in truth is a life expended in God's service. "To do righteousness and justice is desired by the LORD more than sacrifice [outward forms of worship]" (Prov. 21:3 NASB). Those who worship in truth give God the sacrifice he desires.

Second, not only does worship in truth give God the sacrifice he wants, but it also does so without hypocrisy. It is sincere.

A friend rose to speak in a Sunday morning service. "It's easier to sing a lie than speak it," he began. Dead silence! Had we been singing a lie? Had we been singing love songs to God while clinging to resentment? Were we extolling his holiness but holding back our tithes, failing to discipline our children, or refusing to love our mates? If so, our corporate worship was in falsehood, not truth. In summary, don't sing a lie. It grieves the Holy Spirit.

The Cross

The cross tells us everything we need to know about worship. There Jesus worshipped in spirit and truth. In addition, he worshipped his Father for us. He also demonstrated the love and mercy of God, to which all true worship is a response. The cross exhibits three dimensions of worship.

- At the cross Jesus modeled worship in spirit and in truth.
- At the cross Jesus atoned for our failure to worship in spirit and in truth.
- At the cross Jesus showed us why we should worship God in spirit and in truth.

Let's examine these one at a time.

Modeled Worship

First, the Old Testament told us about the worship God desires. But the cross *shows* us this worship. In terms of worship, the cross is God's great "show, don't tell."

Remember, the Old Covenant worshippers brought animal sacrifices to the priest. The worshipper then laid his hands on the sacrifice to confirm that the animal would be put to death in his place. But this worship was always inadequate. No matter how hard the Israelite tried, he could not give God the perfect heart-obedience that is true worship.

The worship offered at the cross was something new. In contrast to the Old Covenant, Christ was both worshipper and priest. He was a high priest offering a perfect sacrifice, and in his case the sacrifice was not bulls and goats, it was his own body. At the cross the priest, rather than the animal, was consumed by the fire of God's wrath (Heb. 12:29). That is why, when Christ came into the world, he said: "Sacrifice and offering you did not desire, but a body you prepared for me; with burnt offerings and sin offerings you were not pleased. Then I said, 'Here I am—it is written about me in the scroll—I have come to do your will, O God'" (Heb. 10:5–7).

What glorious truth! There was Jesus, his body strung out on a Roman cross, showing us the worship God seeks. Nothing less will satisfy. The cross fulfilled every prophetic exhortation to worship God in truth mentioned in the above paragraphs. Every Old Testament sacrifice predicted and awaited this worship.

For example, Jesus' cross fulfilled Micah 6:6–8. There Jesus practiced the love of justice, loving-kindness, and the great humility that the prophet said God looked for in true worshippers.

The cross also expressed the humility of Psalm 51:17. Jesus humbled himself, worshipping God with infinite contrition for our sins.[10]

In contrast to Saul, at the cross Jesus gave God the obedience that characterizes all true worshippers. Jesus obeyed the prophet's injunction: "To obey is better than sacrifice, and to heed is better than the fat of rams" (1 Sam. 15:22).

Every Old Testament exhortation to worship God found its fulfillment at the cross. There Jesus gave his Father the worship that he'd always wanted—a life of perfect obedience proceeding from a heart inflamed with love for him.

Imputed Worship

On the cross Jesus atoned for our inability to worship God in spirit and truth. He worshipped for us. Hallelujah! God imputes Christ's perfect worship to all who believe.

This is why many churches begin their corporate worship with confession of sin. It reminds us that we have not worshipped in spirit and truth during the week, that we need Christ's forgiveness before we enter into corporate singing, and that by faith we can receive his perfect worship imputed to us so we can worship God pleasingly.

When some thought of inadequacy overtakes you during worship, remind yourself of this truth: "At the cross, Jesus worshipped for me. I am free. By faith in his shed blood I can worship from the context of an imperfect life, and I will be acceptable to the Father." All of my failing to worship God in spirit and in truth was punished at the cross.

The Ground of Worship

Christ's cross is the reason and ground for our worship. As we have seen, there is nothing to worship God about until he discloses himself to us. Earlier I quoted Michael Horton's statement that worship is "dialogical," i.e., worship is a *response* to God's revelation. Where do we find the revelation that produces worship? The cross is the Bible's greatest revelation of God's goodness and mercy. In other words, the more we see God's goodness and our bankruptcy at the cross, the greater our capacity for worship. God initiates worship by revealing himself, and the cross is the pinnacle of all worship-inducing revelation.

Romans 12:1–2 stands on this truth. The first eleven chapters of Romans lay out the atonement (the work of the cross) in detail. Then, the first verse of chapter 12 mandates a response. "Therefore, I urge you, brothers, *in view of God's mercy* [the cross], to offer your bodies as living sacrifices, holy and pleasing to God—this is your spiritual act of worship" (Rom. 12:1, emphasis mine).

Paul's connection is simple. The first eleven chapters exalted Christ crucified. There at the cross God revealed his holiness, his righteousness, and his mercy. In response to this love, Paul is saying, "Now you do the same. Give God the worship he seeks. Offer your own bodies as a living sacrifice. Worship God in spirit and truth. Worship in response to his love not just duty."

The highest form of biblical worship is a response to the mercies revealed at the cross. In Revelation 5:9 the saints sing the "new song" for the first time in the New Testament. It is a glorious song of exuberant spiritual worship, and it only happens after the worshippers see the "Lamb, looking as if it had been slain" (Rev. 5:6). The vision of the slain Lamb, standing gloriously because of his willingness to die, always inspires the new song of worship.

Application

This chapter has several important applications. First, if the mercy of God revealed at the cross is the ground of worship, and if we want people to respond in corporate worship to God, then our corporate worship music should be cross-centered. In other words, the lyrics in our worship music should be about the cross. They should speak of human depravity, Christ's bloody sacrifice, God's infinite river of ever-flowing love, and the cost of our propitiation.

But as we saw in chapter 1, this is not the subject of most contemporary worship music, and so our worship suffers. The love of God is a constant subject in our church services, but because we do not sing about our desperate plight in sin, there is little context by which to understand and value that love. There is little revelation to respond to. Vibrant corporate worship is a *response* to preaching and singing about the truths revealed at the cross.

Second, it reminds us that the entire Sunday service is worship. It has become fashionable to speak of the singing as worship in distinction from the preaching of the Word. But the cross tells us that our daily obedience is the worship that God most ardently seeks. If this is true, then the reading of Scripture and the sermon is the most important part of public worship. Therefore, it is an error to separate the singing from the preaching when we think of worship. True worshippers eagerly listen to God's Word so that they can go home and obey it.

It is also a mistake to pick your church based only on the music. The quality and content of the preaching should be the first factor because it, rather than music, is most apt to make you the kind of worshipper God seeks. The goose bumps that proceed from the music satisfy the flesh and are not wrong. But the obedience that proceeds from Word-induced conviction satisfies God's desire to be worshipped.

Third, the principles of this chapter remind us that emotions matter to the subject of worship. Normal biblical worship should proceed from and affect the emotional life. I am not saying that we need to worship our emotions, as some do. We worship God. But as Jonathan Edwards insightfully argued in his masterpiece, *Religious Affections*, the Bible is an emotion-wrought book. If we claim to be led by his Spirit but remain stoic, we probably are not being led by the Spirit.

Nothing stirs the emotions in worship like the truths revealed by the cross as laid down in the preceding chapters. Preach the cross and sing the cross, and the wells of your emotional life will overflow. "The duty of singing praises to God, seems to be appointed wholly to excite and express religious affections [Christian emotions]," noted Edwards. "No other reason can be assigned, why we should express ourselves to God in verse, rather than in prose, and do it with music, but only, that such is our nature and frame, that these things have a tendency to move our affections [emotions]."[11]

But having said this, the opposite is also true. Worship music can be dangerous. Its melodic beauty can stir the emotions without any tip of the hat to truth. This felt emotional response can deceive us into the conviction that we have worshipped. But if the will has not been moved to obey, there is little worship in spirit and in truth.

Therefore, the stirring of the emotions is good if it is a response to truth. Emotions matter, and they serve us if they respond to the truth conveyed by the lyrics. This is why, when musicians choose songs, they should put the emphasis on the lyrics.

Last, the greatest obstacle to rich corporate worship for many of us is guilt and inadequacy. None of us has ever worshipped God adequately. Only one Man has. He did so naked, on a dry, splinter-studded Golgotha cross two thousand years ago. But if you believe, he will impute that perfection to you. What joy! What freedom! We can now confidently approach his throne of grace and mercy, not on our merits but his, worshipping freely from blood-cleansed consciences.

Conclusion

We should fear the worship wars. They miss the point. It is not about the style of music. When we make this an issue, we prove that we don't understand the worship Jesus modeled from the cross—worship in spirit and truth.

The cross was Christ's spiritual act of worship. He sacrificed what the Father really wanted, his life. He worshipped in spirit and in truth, and he did it in our place. To the degree that we see the love, mercy, compassion, and justice displayed there, our corporate singing and our entire lives will be a joyful response that will deeply please the Father's desire to be worshipped in spirit and truth.

Notes

Preface

1. John R. Stott, *The Cross of Christ* (Downers Grove, Ill.: InterVarsity Press, 1986), 204.

Chapter 1: The Centrality of the Cross

1. *The New Encyclopedia of Christian Quotations* (Grand Rapids: Baker, 2000), 244.

2. James Denney, *The Atonement and the Modern Mind* (London: Hodder and Stoughton, 1903), 1–2.

3. A note on Calvinism: The writings of John Calvin and his successors seem to me to be the best summarization of biblical teaching available. But having said that, I want to assert that my identification is with Christ not Calvinism. My main concern is with the Bible's teaching. My secondary concern is with Calvinism and other leaders of church history.

4. Brian Edwards, *Revival* (Darlington, U.K.: Evangelical Press, 1990), 107–8.

5. P. T. Forsyth, *The Cruciality of the Cross* (1909; reprint, Cumbria, U.K.: Paternoster Press, 1997), 23.

177

6. *The International Standard Bible Encyclopaedia,* vol. 2 (Grand Rapids: Eerdmans, 1976), 761.

7. P. T. Forsyth, quoted in Stott, *The Cross of Christ,* 43.

8. *The New Encyclopedia of Christian Quotations,* 806.

9. Mark Noll, taken from D. A. Carson, *Worship by the Book* (Grand Rapids: Zondervan, 2002), 32.

10. One wonderful exception to this that I am personally aware of is the music of Sovereign Grace Ministries in Gaithersburg, Maryland.

Chapter 2: Foundations

1. For more details read the excellent article in *The International Standard Bible Encyclopaedia,* ed. James Orr (1939; reprint, Grand Rapids: Eerdmans, 1976), 760.

2. See Louis Berkhof, *The History of Christian Doctrines* (1937; reprint, London: Banner of Truth, 1969), 165–98.

3. The work of Anselm in the twelfth century helped to recover this wonderful doctrine. His book *Cur Deus Homo* was a great turning point in the recovery of the substitutionary atonement.

4. Old Testament: Leviticus 1–6; Isaiah 53; Psalm 22. New Testament: 1 Peter 2:24; Hebrews 9:28; 2 Corinthians 5:14, 21; Galatians 3:14.

5. Denney, *The Atonement and the Modern Mind,* 82, quoted in Stott, *The Cross of Christ,* 133.

6. Calvin's commentary on the gospel according to Saint John, quoted in Stott, *The Cross of Christ,* 206.

Chapter 3: God 101

1. A. W. Tozer, *The Knowledge of the Holy* (New York: Harper and Row, 1961), 9.

2. Ibid.

3. For a devastating argument on the importance of the intellect in spiritual development, see Jonathan Edwards's sermon entitled "Christian Knowledge" in his *Works,* vol. 2, 157–62.

4. *The Harmony of the Divine Attributes* by William Bates was a great aid to me at this juncture.

5. Wayne Grudem, *Systematic Theology* (Grand Rapids: Zondervan, 1994), 568.

6. Stott, *The Cross of Christ*, 211.

7. Carnegie Simpson, quoted in Stott, *The Cross of Christ*, 88.

8. J. I. Packer, *Knowing God* (Downers Grove, Ill.: InterVarsity Press, 1973), 118.

9. Ibid., 137.

10. A. W. Pink, *The Attributes of God* (Grand Rapids: Baker, 1975), 77.

11. J. R. White, *The God Who Justifies* (Minneapolis: Bethany, 2001), 46.

12. Stott, *The Cross of Christ*, 221.

13. Denney, *The Atonement and the Modern Mind*, 84–85.

14. A. W. Pink, *The Sovereignty of God* (Edinburgh: Banner of Truth, 1993), 25.

15. See John Musser, *The Infidel* (Nashville: Broadman & Holman, 2001).

Chapter 4: The Worst of Sinners

1. J. C. Ryle, *Holiness* (1879; reprint, Darlington, England: Evangelical Press, 1979), 8.

2. Elizabeth Nickson, *World*, 13 April 2002, 13.

3. See David Myers, *The Inflated Self* (New York: Seabury, 1980), 22–23.

4. *U.S. News and World Report*, 31 March 1997, 18.

5. See Barna Research online at www.barna.org. To make these figures accurate I added only half of the average ratings to the average or above average. If I had added all the average ratings to the average or above average category the figures would be even more distorted.

6. See David Myers's college textbook *Social Psychology*, 5th ed. (New York: McGraw Hill, 1996).

7. Paul Billheimer, *Don't Waste Your Sorrows* (Fort Washington, Pa.: Christian Literature Crusade, 1977), 33.

8. Leon Morris, *The Atonement* (Downers Grove, Ill.: InterVarsity Press, 1983), 153.

9. Blaise Pascal, *Pensees* (New York: Washington Square Press, 1965).

10. John Piper, *The Pleasures of God* (Sisters, Ore.: Multnomah, 2000), 276.

11. See 2 Corinthians 11:22 and following for an intimate description of *some* of the apostle's sufferings. This list did not include most of his sufferings recorded in Acts, which had not yet occurred.

12. George Smeaton, *Paul's Doctrine of the Atonement: Taken from "The Doctrine of the Atonement According to the Apostles."* Index created by Christian Classics Foundation (electronic ed. based on Hendrickson reprint of 1870 ed.) (Simpsonville, S.C.: Christian Classics Foundation, 1996), 86.

13. Stott, *The Cross of Christ,* 161.

14. Smeaton, *Paul's Doctrine of the Atonement,* 48.

15. Packer, *Knowing God,* 112.

Chapter 5: For God's Glory

1. Millard Erickson, *Systematic Theology* (Grand Rapids: Baker, 1983), 352.

2. John Hannah, *To God Be the Glory* (Wheaton, Ill.: Crossway Books, 2000), 9.

3. Daniel Fuller, *The Unity of the Bible* (Grand Rapids: Zondervan, 1992), 206–7.

4. I have written extensively on this theme elsewhere. See my book *For His Glory: God's Ultimate Purpose and Why It Matters to the Church* (Spokane: Pinnacle Press, 1998).

5. See Jonathan Edwards's *Unpublished Essay on the Trinity,* www.jonathanedwards.com.

6. Also see Isaiah 44:23 and Psalm 79:9.

7. *The Works of Jonathan Edwards,* vol. I (Edinburgh: Banner of Truth, 1974), 110.

8. Dr. Martyn Lloyd-Jones, *Saved in Eternity* (Wheaton, Ill.: Crossway, 1988).

9. Notice: Jesus loved us by putting God ahead of us. Had people's happiness been Christ's first objective, he would have fallen short of God's glory, and we would be lost in our sins. Thank God that Jesus was impassioned with zeal for his Father's glory.

10. David Morgan, quoted in Edwards, *Revival*, 57.

11. Paul Hattaway Yun, *The Heavenly Man* (Grand Rapids: Kregel, 2003).

12. Death to self is the umbrella means, but there are many sub-means that fit under this category. For example, Jesus glorified God by completing the work God gave him (John 17:4); Abraham glorified God by believing (Romans 4:20); miracles glorify God (John 2:11).

13. Arnold Dallimore, *George Whitefield*, vol. 2 (Edinburgh: Banner of Truth, 1970), 522.

14. Ibid., 252–53.

Chapter 6: Crucified Flesh

1. This is a major premise of Jonathan Edwards's *Freedom of the Will*. Ultimately everyone's will is enslaved to the pursuit of happiness by God's design.

2. Vernon J. Bourke, ed., *The Essential Augustine* (New York: New American Library, 1964), 151.

3. *The Works of Jonathan Edwards*, vol. 2, 145.

4. I am not saying that self-discipline is ever completely ended. It is always there, but it is an increasingly smaller part of Christian motivation as we see Christ more and more.

5. A series of biblical texts make this point. See Psalm 135:18; Romans 1:22; 2 Corinthians 3:18; 1 John 3:2; Isaiah 44:15–25; Exodus 32:7; 2 Kings 17:15; and Psalm 115:8.

6. Stott, *The Cross of Christ*, 83.

7. Brian Edwards, *Revival* (Durham, U.K.: Evangelical Press, 1998), 116.

8. Golgotha was probably the city garbage site. It was the fitting place to execute criminals.

9. A popular definition of meekness is "strength under control," but this does not seem to go far enough.

10. John Brown, *John Bunyan* (Hamden, Conn.: Archon, 1969), 178.

11. Piper, *The Pleasures of God*, 16.

Chapter 7: God's Spiritual Boot Camp

1. First, Peter was Satan's mouthpiece (Matthew 16:23). Later, Jesus allowed the devil to sift Peter (Luke 22:31–34).

2. Paul mentions other weapons in Ephesians 6:13–17 and 2 Corinthians 10:1–6. But they depend upon these three basic weapons.

3. "It [Ps. 22] may have actually been repeated word by word by our Lord when hanging on the tree; it would be too bold to say that it was so, but even a casual reader may see that it might have been," Charles Spurgeon, *Treasury of David* (Grand Rapids: Baker, 1978), 365. "In short, there is no doubt that Christ, in uttering this exclamation upon the cross ["My God, my God why have you forsaken me], manifestly showed, that although David here bewails his own distresses, this psalm was composed under the influence of the Spirit of prophecy concerning David's King and Lord," John Calvin, *Commentary on Psalms* (Ages Software), 346. "It [Psalm 22] contains those deep, sublime, and heavy sufferings of Christ when agonizing in the midst of the terrors and pangs of divine wrath and death, which surpass all human thought and comprehension." Martin Luther, quoted by Spurgeon, *Treasury of David*, vol. I (Grand Rapids: Baker), 377.

4. http://www.allinclusivechrist.org/experiences/ (20 May 2003).

5. Go back to chapter 2 for a refresher.

6. Pierre Van Paassen, *A Crown of Fire* (New York: Scribner, 1960), 296–97.

7. Ibid., 297.

8. *The Works of Jonathan Edwards*, vol. 2, 152.

9. I don't mean perfect obedience. That is impossible. I mean the clear conscience mentioned by Paul in I Corinthians 4:3–4. An obedient believer is one with no unconfessed sin.

Chapter 8: I Will Boast No More

1. Jerry Bridges, *The Gospel for Real Life* (Colorado Springs: NavPress, 2002), 129.

2. See George Smeaton, *Paul's Doctrine of the Atonement* for a detailed discussion of this interpretation of this verse.

3. For a detailed description read 2 Corinthians 11:22ff.

4. See Philippians 3:5–6 for the details. Paul was talented. Paul had achieved great things, but these things had to die in order for Paul to know Christ.

5. A. A. Bonar and R. McCheyne, *Memoir and Remains of R. M. Mc-Cheyne* (1947; reprint, Chicago: Moody Press, 1996), 265–66. Index created by Christian Classics Foundation. Published in electronic form by Christian Classics Foundation.

Chapter 9: The Foolishness of God's Wisdom

1. Stephen Charnock, *The Existence and Attributes of God*, vol. 1 (1853; reprint, Grand Rapids: Baker, 1979), 507.

2. For more details on this subject see my book *For His Glory*. Also, chapter 5 discussed this subject in some detail.

3. Piper, *The Pleasures of God*, 272.

4. Stott, *The Cross of Christ*, 224.

5. Packer, *Knowing God*, 90.

6. Barna Research Online, http://www.barna.org/cgi-bin/pagepress release.asp?PressreleaseID=138&ReferenceA (6 May 2003).

7. Ibid.

8. Business marketing and polling principles might be of some help if they are clearly subordinated to the evangelistic means assumed by the Bible.

9. James Denney, *The Death of Christ* (1902; reprint, New Canaan, Conn.: Keats Publishing, 1981), 7.

10. Stott, *The Cross of Christ*, 351.

Chapter 10: The Supreme Sufferer in the Universe

1. Scott Manetsch, "The Saint Bartholomew's Day Massacre," *Christian History Magazine*, issue 71, 9.

2. Paul Billheimer, *Destined for the Throne* (Fort Washington, Pa.: CLC, 1975), 29.

3. C. S. Lewis, *The Problem of Pain* (New York: Macmillan, 1962), 84.

4. Ibid., 93.

5. William Gurnall, 17th century Puritan.

6. See 2 Corinthians 11:22ff for a catalog of his stupendous suffering for the gospel.

7. Billheimer, *Don't Waste Your Sorrows*, 36.

8. Phillip Schaff, *Church History*, vol. 6. Ages Software edition.

9. *The New Encyclopedia of Christian Quotations*, 983.

Chapter 11: The Heart of Worship

1. See Psalm 28:2; Psalm 44:20; Psalm 63:4; Psalm 77:2; Psalm 88:9; Psalm 134:20.

2. See Psalm 47:1; Psalm 98:8.

3. See Exodus 15; Psalm 30:11; Psalm 149:3; Psalm 150:4.

4. See Psalm 20:5; Psalm 33:3; Psalm 42:4; Psalm 47:5; Psalm 100:1, for example.

5. Charnock, *The Existence and Attributes of God.*

6. Don't try. I made this term up.

7. Michael Horton, *A Better Way* (Grand Rapids: Baker, 2002), 26.

8. God is merciful toward sinners, but he is never tolerant of sin. There is a difference.

9. Iain Murray, *Jonathan Edwards* (Edinburgh: Banner of Truth, 1987), 442.

10. He did not need to repent of his own sin. He was sinless.

11. *The Works of Jonathan Edwards*, vol. 1, 242.

Wm. P. Farley is the pastor of Grace Christian Fellowship, a nondenominational evangelical church in Spokane, Washington. His articles have appeared in *Discipleship Journal, Focus on the Family, The Pentecostal Evangel, Pulpit Helps,* and *Enrichment Journal.* He is also the author of *For His Glory.* He has been married to Judy, his best friend, for thirty-one years. They have three daughters, two sons, and six grandsons.